Quality 20,20

407899

371.782
How

S0-BND-439

407899

HOW CAN SCHOOL VIOLENCE BE PREVENTED?

Other books in the At Issue series:

HOW CAN SCHOOL VIOLENCE BE PREVENTED?

Scott Barbour, *Book Editor*

Bruce Glassman, *Vice President*
Bonnie Szumski, *Publisher*
Helen Cothran, *Managing Editor*

GREENHAVEN PRESS
An imprint of Thomson Gale, a part of The Thomson Corporation

SHELBYVILLE-SHELBY COUNTY
PUBLIC LIBRARY

Detroit • New York • San Francisco • San Diego • New Haven, Conn.
Waterville, Maine • London • Munich

© 2005 Thomson Gale, a part of The Thomson Corporation.

Thomson and Star Logo are trademarks and Gale and Greenhaven Press are registered trademarks used herein under license.

For more information, contact
Greenhaven Press
27500 Drake Rd.
Farmington Hills, MI 48331-3535
Or you can visit our Internet site at http://www.gale.com

ALL RIGHTS RESERVED.
No part of this work covered by the copyright hereon may be reproduced or used in any form or by any means—graphic, electronic, or mechanical, including photocopying, recording, taping, Web distribution or information storage retrieval systems—without the written permission of the publisher.

Every effort has been made to trace the owners of copyrighted material.

LIBRARY OF CONGRESS CATALOGING-IN-PUBLICATION DATA

How can school violence be prevented? / Scott Barbour, book editor.
   p. cm. — (At issue)
Includes bibliographical references and index.
ISBN 0-7377-2382-3 (lib. : alk. paper) — ISBN 0-7377-2383-1 (pbk. : alk. paper)
   1. School violence—United States—Prevention. I. Barbour, Scott, 1963– .
II. At issue (San Diego, Calif.)
LB3013.32 .H69 2005
371.7'82—dc22
                                                 2004042514

Printed in the United States of America

Contents

Introduction

Since the mid-1990s, America has witnessed a string of shootings in its schools. The deadliest of these tragedies occurred on April 20, 1999, when students Eric Harris and Dylan Klebold went on a massive rampage at Columbine High School in Littleton, Colorado, killing twelve students and one teacher and wounding twenty-three others before killing themselves. Fortunately, there have been no subsequent shootings on the scale of Columbine. However, school shootings do continue to take place. For example, on April 24, 2003, James Sheets, a fourteen-year-old student at Red Lion Junior High School in Pennsylvania, shot and killed the school's principal before turning his gun around and killing himself. On September 24, 2003, fifteen-year-old John Jason McLaughlin brought a gun to Rocori High School in Cold Spring, Minnesota, and shot two students, apparently at random. One victim died soon after being shot; the other survived for about a month before succumbing to his injuries. These are just two of many examples of deadly school violence since Columbine. These incidents, especially Columbine, have prompted a national debate over the nature, causes, and potential solutions to such violence.

Many surveys support the impression created by these shootings that violence is a problem in the schools. A report by Rand, a public policy research institute, finds that during a given school year, about one-half of middle and high school students report at least one incident of attacks, fights, theft, larceny, or vandalism. In addition, 7 to 8 percent of high school students report that they have been threatened or injured with a weapon on school property. A survey of school principals conducted by the U.S. Department of Education found that in one school year, 10 percent of schools experienced at least one serious violent crime, and 66 percent of schools experienced at least one less serious violent crime, including fighting without a weapon, vandalism, and theft. In the same study, a survey of students revealed that 18 percent had been threatened with a beating, 13 percent had been attacked with a weapon, and 11 percent had experienced at least one act of violence at school, including being robbed or threatened with a weapon.

Many social commentators caution against exaggerating the problem of school violence. Some insist that excessive media coverage of school shootings—combined with the dramatic and horrific nature of the crimes—has created the belief that such incidents are on the rise when they are actually declining. According to the School Violence Resource Center, an organization that works to reduce violence in schools, deaths from school violence decreased from fifty-six in the 1991–1992 school year to twenty-two in 2000–2001. A child's chance of dying from homicide at school is 1 in 1.7 million. In fact, the risk of being killed by violence at school is less than the risk of dying from an automobile accident, influenza, or an accidental fall. As stated by sociology professor Joel Best, the "evidence flatly contradicted the claims that there was a wave, trend, or epidemic of school violence [at the time of Columbine]. In other words, the wave of school shootings was a phantom—that is, a nonexistent trend."

Although disagreement exists about the severity of the problem, all agree that just one school shooting is a horrible tragedy and that schools should be made as safe as possible. To this end, school administrators, policy makers, and concerned parents have attempted to devise ways to prevent school violence. Some of these measures have targeted society at large. For example, some have called for stricter gun control laws to keep young people from getting access to deadly weapons. Others have demanded that the entertainment industry tone down the violence in its movies, music videos, and video games, fearing that such depictions of pretend violence inure children and teens to the consequences of real violence. Still others call for more parental involvement in children's lives or a greater emphasis on religious and moral values at home and in the schools. Another set of solutions focuses on the schools themselves. Schools nationwide have increased their security efforts, installing cameras, metal detectors, and increased security personnel. Some districts have adopted zero-tolerance policies, which provide mandatory, harsh punishments for any student caught possessing a weapon or making threats of violence. In addition, because many school shooters were reportedly bullied prior to lashing out, many schools have instituted programs designed to reduce student bullying.

One school-based solution to the problem of violence that has proven particularly controversial is student profiling. Experts believe that students who act out violently share certain characteristics. For example, they are likely to be interested in weapons, be bullied or be a bully, and be alienated from the popular group at school. By creating a profile of a typical school shooter, it may be possible to identify students who are at risk for committing a violent crime before they do so. To assist in this effort, the National School Safety Center (NSSC), an organization dedicated to reducing school violence, has created a "Checklist of Characteristics of Youth Who Have Caused School-Associated Violent Deaths." The list contains twenty items, including those listed above as well as other warning signs such as "Displays cruelty to animals," "Habitually makes violent threats when angry," and "Has witnessed or been a victim of abuse or neglect in the home." The American Psychological Association, a professional organization for psychologists, and the U.S. Department of Education have created similar lists of warning signs.

Many experts criticize the use of checklists and profiles to identify students at risk of violence. They argue that the traits and behaviors listed on the checklists could describe nearly any teen. For example, the NSSC list includes "Is often depressed and/or has significant mood swings." However, mood swings are certainly not unusual during adolescence. Other items in the list include "Consistently prefers TV shows, movies, or music expressing violent themes and acts" and "Is on the fringe of his/her peer group with few or no close friends." In short, while some warning signs are indeed clear and undeniable signs of trouble, others could describe large numbers of teens, the vast majority of whom would never consider bringing a gun to school. In addition, critics contend, the use of such checklists has the potential to punish and stigmatize teens who simply differ from the norm. After all, teens naturally experiment with their identities and seek to assert themselves as unique individuals. Opponents charge that checklists simply hamper creative self-expression and enforce a code of conformity on the young. For these reasons, many agencies and individuals, including the U.S. Secret Service, have expressed opposition to profiling. As Rand concludes:

> Although a great deal is known about early warning signs of violent behavior, the truth is that many students fit these "profiles" and only very few will ever commit a violent act. Hence, many students who will never commit violence are labeled as potentially violent. The label itself can lead to stigmatization and, if linked with a segregated group intervention, the labeling can also significantly limit the opportunities of the identified students.

The attempt to create a profile of a school shooter, along with the criticism such efforts evoke, makes clear that school violence is a complex problem immune to simple solutions. While all agree that warning signs for violence exist, these warning signs apply to nearly every teen, and there is no way to predict where and when circumstances will combine to compel a young person to bring a gun to school and begin shooting. In *At Issue: How Can School Violence Be Prevented?* authors examine this difficult issue and debate the best way to head off tragedies similar to those that have occurred in Columbine, Red Lion, Rocori, and other schools across the nation.

1

Antibullying Programs Can Prevent School Violence

Rita Healy, Marc Hequet, and Collette McKenna-Parker

Rita Healy, Marc Hequet, and Collette McKenna-Parker are freelance writers who have reported for Time *magazine and other publications.*

Besides being cruel in itself, bullying is often the precursor to serious acts of school violence. More than two-thirds of perpetrators of school shootings were bullied prior to lashing out. Schools nationwide have instituted innovative and effective programs to reduce the bullying that can so often escalate into tragedy. The most effective programs are those that change school culture to make teasing and harassment unacceptable.

The 450 freshmen and sophomores gathered in the auditorium of Stephenson High School in Stone Mountain, Ga., are contemplating a red poster with a drawing of a large angry face and the word BULLY. That poster and two others, marked VICTIM and BYSTANDER, form the backdrop for the action onstage. Victor—with his black beret and long, stringy hair that scream "Victim!"—is enduring a stream of abuse from Brad. "I can call you anything I want because I'm a man and you're a punk sissy nerd!" Brad shouts after stealing Victor's hat. The audience laughs hysterically. "We don't want punk sissy nerds like you hanging around our school. Right?" asks Brad, prompting the watching kids to chant "Punk sissy nerd" in an unconscious display of bystander cravenness. But when the play is over, the students are more reflective. "It was really good," says Shina Mills, a sophomore. "It helps teenagers not to resolve problems on their own but to get help."

A skit about big bad bullies may seem ludicrously quaint against the backdrop of teen shootings like the one last week [March 22, 2001] in El Cajon, Calif. [in which a student wounded five people]. But the professional production, part of the local school district's efforts to combat bullying, seeks in a small way to change the weekly headlines. More and more schools around the country are implementing antibullying policies. New laws in Georgia, New Hampshire and Vermont require them, and

Rita Healy, Marc Hequet, and Collette McKenna-Parker, "Let Bullies Beware," *Time*, vol. 157, April 2, 2001, p. 46. Copyright © 2001 by Time, Inc. Reproduced by permission.

Colorado, home to the Columbine school massacre,[1] is debating a measure. Skeptics say such legislation is fruitless and serves merely as a platform for politicians to display their practiced empathy. But some innovative programs around the country are showing concrete results that challenge the laissez-faire mentality that, after all, kids will be kids.

That bullying is a destructive force is not in dispute. Last fall [2000] the National Threat Assessment Center, run by the U.S. Secret Service, found that in more than two-thirds of 37 recent school shootings, the attackers felt "persecuted, bullied, threatened, attacked or injured." And bullying is why more than 160,000 children skip school every day, according to the National Association of School Psychologists.

"We need to change the climate so that most kids feel it's inappropriate to tease and harass."

Georgia began its pioneering efforts to legislate against bullying after two school tragedies. In 1994 Brian Head, a chubby, bespectacled 15-year-old who had been taunted for years, broke when a classmate at Etowah High School in Woodstock slapped him. He shouted, "I can't take it anymore!," pulled out a gun and shot himself in the head. Four years later, Josh Belluardo was punched in the head—and killed—by a bully who also attended Etowah. The next year, Georgia passed a three-strikes-and-you're-out policy. After three bullying offenses, middle and high school students may be shipped to a school for problem kids.

That kind of heavy hand has its opponents. William Pollack, a psychologist who wrote *Real Boys' Voices*, an exploration of boyhood, contends that such a punitive approach criminalizes childhood behavior and fails to address the root causes of bullying. Dorothy Espelage, an assistant professor at the University of Illinois at Urbana-Champaign who co-authored a study on bullies, favors a comprehensive approach. "As soon as you pull a bully out of a school, another will take his place," she says. A deeper shift in school culture is required, she argues, because ultimately peer groups, not individuals, promote an ethic of aggression. She adds, "We need to change the climate so that most kids feel it's inappropriate to tease and harass."

That's what McNair Elementary in Hazelwood, Mo., attempts to do. In 1992 principal Peggy Dolan instituted a program to unteach kids what many had learned at home—that they should fight back when bullied. Instead, students are instructed to respond verbally, first with "I don't like what you said to me," then "I'm going to ask you to stop" and, if necessary, "I'm going to get help." Victims fill out a form describing the incident to a teacher or counselor. The issue is taken to peer mediation, and the offender is encouraged to sign an agreement not to bully.

Before the program went into effect, Dolan dealt with 55 fights a year; now she averages six. Also, the school's standardized math and reading

---

1. On April 20, 1999, students Eric Harris and Dylan Klebold went on a shooting rampage at Columbine High School in Littleton, Colorado, killing twelve students, one teacher, and themselves. They had reportedly been bullied and harassed prior to the incident.

scores have risen from the 40th to the 60th percentile—in part, she thinks, because students are better able to focus on their studies.

At Central York Middle School in Pennsylvania, incidents of fistfights have also declined—to four so far this school year [2001], compared with 17 last year [2000]—after students in Grades 6 through 8 signed anti-teasing pledges and were instructed how to manage their anger. Bullies were required to offer "active apologies," detailing how they would modify their behavior.

Testifying last week before a Colorado legislative committee on education, Sherry Workman, principal of Laurel Elementary in Fort Collins, noted that behavior infractions fell 66% after she implemented various "bullyproofing" initiatives at her school. The younger children, for instance, are coached in how to walk confidently past older kids who are talking aggressively. Grades 2 through 4 undergo "Be Cool" training, in which counselors present provocative scenarios and ask students to decide between a "hot response" and a "cool response." The latter choice wins praise for the kids.

Bullying is often performance art. Peter Fonagy, a psychologist who helped develop an antibullying model popular in Topeka, Kans., schools, believes that bullies and their victims usually make up no more than 10% to 20% of any school population. "The whole drama is supported by the bystander," says Fonagy. "The theater can't take place if there's no audience." Seeds University Elementary School in Los Angeles uses "equity guidelines" to target both bullies and bystanders. Parents and students sign contracts at the beginning of the year stipulating that no child may be put down for academic performance, appearance, family composition or gender, among other things. When an incident occurs—for example, some boys tried to pull down another boy's pants—bystanders are also sent to after-school mediation.

While the Seeds program involves parents, many others don't. "Research shows that the success of any program is 60% grounded in whether the same kinds of approaches are used at home," says Pollack. Sometimes parents need to be educated. When Debora Smith discovered that her two boys at Wolfpit Elementary School in Norwalk, Conn., were being bullied, she took action—by arming them with a hammer and screwdriver. Luckily, the school principal found the weapons in the kids' knapsacks before any harm was done.

2

Antibullying Programs Are Ineffective and Unnecessary

Matt Labash

Matt Labash is a senior writer at the Weekly Standard, *a conservative magazine.*

Social scientists and educators have developed school-based anti-bullying programs in an effort to combat the perceived problem of school violence. These programs are unnecessary because, contrary to popular belief, school violence is decreasing rather than increasing. They are also ineffective because they do not impart useful tools for responding to bullying but simply teach children how to identify and express their feelings. Several rigorous studies have failed to prove that such programs actually reduce bullying. Antibullying programs may do more harm than good by leaving children even less prepared for the interpersonal conflicts that have always been a normal, albeit unpleasant, part of school life.

In 1999, [Peter] Yarrow's [of the folk group Peter, Paul & Mary, or PPM] life and, consequently, the lives of millions of American schoolchildren were transformed. At the Kerrville Folk Festival, Yarrow heard a hit country song entitled "Don't Laugh At Me," which he decided to turn into an anti-bullying anthem, thus launching a movement. While the lyrics had been written by somebody else, they are PPM-pitch-perfect: "I'm a little boy with glasses, the one they call a geek /A little girl who never smiles cause I have braces on my teeth / and I know how it feels / to cry myself to sleep." From there, things really get maudlin, spiraling into the chorus: "Don't laugh at me / Don't call me names / Don't get your pleasure from my pain . . ." Yarrow has said he "shed a tear" the first time he heard the song. It reminded him of his own painful experiences being bullied by a football player: "He would call me [names]. That was very humiliating," Yarrow said. He was in college at the time.

The song, ideally suited to the trademark Yarrow whine, which resembles the slow leaking of air from a balloon, has been rerecorded by Peter, Paul & Mary and incorporated into a video and CD, the latter of which

Matt Labash, "Beating Up on Bullies," *Weekly Standard*, vol. 8, February 24, 2003, p. 23. Copyright © 2003 by News Corporation, Weekly Standard. All rights reserved. Reproduced by permission.

includes other PPM hits like "Weave Me the Sunshine" and "Puff the Magic Dragon." Both the video and CD serve as cornerstones of the "Don't Laugh at Me" curriculum, co-developed by Yarrow's non-profit "Operation Respect" in conjunction with Educators for Social Responsibility and another outfit called Adventures in Peacemaking. The anti-bullying curriculum comes in three incarnations (the Camp Program, Grades 2–5, and Grades 6–8). The materials include festive signs that say things like "Ridicule Free Zone" and "No Dissing Here"—proving that these '60s era holdovers are hip to the kids' lingo, or at least to the lingo they used back in 1992.

While there are any number of similar programs that aim to eradicate bullying in schools, "Don't Laugh At Me" is achieving critical mass. Given away for free, the curriculum has been implemented in over 15,000 schools and summer camps nationwide. The song (which Yarrow calls the "We Shall Overcome" of the anti-bullying movement), the video, and the guides have been given a tremendous push by everyone from state departments of education to the NEA [National Education Association] to the National Association of Elementary School Principals.

A recent "epidemic"

Bullying, of course, is a new phenomenon only if you remember Cain's bludgeoning of Abel as if it were yesterday. Bullies themselves have been the stuff of nearly every great coming of age novel and film since time immemorial. From the Victorian-era Flashman in Tom Brown's *School Days* to the yellow-eyed Scut Farkus in *A Christmas Story*, the bully has served as a source of fear and object of ire, a mettle-tester and very often a muse. But only recently has bullying been treated as an "epidemic"—studied, pathologized, and in some instances criminalized by both the education establishment and lawmakers. The DLAM program in fact grows out of a generation's worth of activism.

While brown cheese and Lutefisk are Scandinavia's most famous exports, anti-bullying propaganda likely comes in a close third. So it has been since Swedish researcher Dan Olweus, the father of the anti-bullying movement, began publishing a steady drip of bullying scholarship from his perch at Bergen University in Norway in the 1970s. Since Olweus was the first person to study both bullies and their victims systematically, many of his conclusions have become articles of faith: everything from the notion that bullying has grown more serious and prevalent, to the assertion that bullies themselves are much likelier than others to have criminal convictions later in life.

Not surprisingly, with a purported increase in bullying—and with millions of dollars now available worldwide to study and implement anti-bullying measures—there has also been a spike in the supply of anti-bullying consultants. Olweus, like many other anti-bullying researchers, doubles as one. If you, as a school principal, feel bullying is a problem (or even if you don't but your school board does), you might be forced to adopt something like Olweus's anti-bullying curriculum.

In promotional materials for the Olweus Bullying Prevention Program—which calls for measures such as holding 20–40 minute-per-week classroom meetings on the subject—it is suggested that you buy a copy of

Olweus's $22.95 book and $30 handbook for each staff member, along with his "Bully/Victim Questionnaire" software at $200 per school. As if that weren't burdensome enough, the materials state that "depending on the school's size," the program "will require a part- or full-time onsite co-ordinator."

Through most of history, no one needed social scientists to tell them kids were cruel, so bullying was considered an unfortunate but inevitable byproduct of school life—like the poor quality of cafeteria food, or the promiscuity of cheerleaders. But it is now a problem that educationists feel they must Seriously Address. Consequently, the anti-bullying movement has fanned out from Scandinavia, taking root in countries like Australia, Canada, and Great Britain.

A simplistic response to school shootings

Though the United States is a relative latecomer, the anti-bullying movement's flourishing in our country can be traced to a specific date: April 20, 1999, the day Eric Harris and Dyland Klebold took the lives of 13 people at Columbine High School. Indeed, in a strange way, school shooters have become the patron saints of the anti-bullying movement, serving as warnings of what happens when bullying goes unchecked. In the current climate, the horrifying specter of mass murder is, if not excused, at least understood—its gravity downgraded so long as the shooter once received a wedgie from the captain of the football team.

Bullying, of course, is a new phenomenon only if you remember Cain's bludgeoning of Abel as if it were yesterday.

Nearly all anti-bullying proponents point to a 2000 Secret Service study reporting that in 37 school shootings since 1974, two-thirds of the attackers said they felt "persecuted, bullied, threatened, attacked or injured." Though Harris and Klebold weren't available to participate in the Secret Service's post-mortem on account of their suicides, there is little doubt they too had been branded outcasts by more popular classmates. But here, uncomfortable though it surely is, the chicken-and-egg question is in order: Were Harris and Klebold sociopaths because they were ostracized, or were they ostracized for being sociopaths?

Not to excuse any unkind behavior on the part of the Columbine jock class—the one that has become the national stand-in for popular kids behaving boorishly—but for a moment, put yourself in their place. If two guys came to your school in goth facepaint, boasting of mutilating animals, spewing hate toward blacks and Jews, and voicing praise for Hitler (all of which either Klebold or Harris is reported to have done preshooting), even from the vantage point of enlightened adulthood, you might not ask them to sit by you on the bus.

Likewise, there's no evidence the simplistic approach of implementing anti-bullying programs can head off such incidents. When Charles "Andy" Williams shot 15 people at Santana High School in Santee, California, in 2001, he, too, claimed he was bullied. But three years before, his school had been the beneficiary of a $123,000 Justice Department anti-bullying grant.

Violence is decreasing

There are, however, bigger problems with taking an increase in school violence as an indicator that bullying is on the rise. To begin with, school violence is decreasing. One statistical analysis after another shows school violence has been on the decline since 1992—a trend that pre-dates our anti-bullying movement by a good six years. Checking the Consumer Product Safety Commission's numbers against those of the National Center for Education Statistics (NCES), one learns that almost as many children were killed by toys such as non-powered scooters and balloons in 2001 (25) as were killed by school-related violence (38 homicides) in 1998–99. In fact, more people were killed by nursery equipment and supplies (51). According to the NCES, nearly every indicator of danger in schools is trending downward: from the number of students who claimed they were robbed, to those who got into fights.

The problem begins with the fact that people can't agree on what bullying is.

Nearly every indicator, that is, except one, which perhaps not coincidentally dovetails with the boom in anti-bullying programs sensitizing our kids to the phenomenon: The NCES reports that from 1999 to 2001, students claiming they had been bullied in the last six months rose from 5 percent to 8 percent. Depending on who's doing the asking and how, that number fluctuates wildly (I found some claims that over 80 percent of children report being victims of bullies). This, of course, is a fundamental shortcoming of anti-bullying research, as even the movement's founder, Olweus, concedes. It relies not on dispassionate and objective scientific observation, but on student self-reporting, which is entirely subjective. If one enters the emotional tsunami that is the psyche of the typical 13-year-old boy or girl, then asks whether anyone in these kids' world is picking on them, it's a fair bet that those bullying numbers will rocket through the stratosphere.

Broad definitions of bullying

The problem begins with the fact that people can't agree on what bullying is. While many would insist—as [Supreme Court] Justice Potter Stewart said of obscenity—they know it when they see it, the results whenever people are forced to define bullying in black and white are laughable. As specified by lawmakers, bullying now encompasses a lot more than Big Johnny pounding the stuffing out of Little Timmy behind the school gym.

The National Conference of State Legislatures estimates that at least 17 states have passed some sort of anti-bullying measure. Here's a sampling of partial definitions: Colorado says bullying "means any written or verbal expression, or physical act or gesture . . . intended to cause distress upon one or more students in school." Oregon defines it as "any act that substantially interferes with a student's educational benefits." Vermont prohibits any physical or verbal hostility directed at, among other things, a student's race or sexual orientation or "marital status" (marital status?). Nevada defines bullying as a "willful act or course of conduct" that "is highly offensive to a reasonable person," which would seem to preclude the Nevada legislature.

Excessive punishments

With lawmakers so willing to institutionalize anti-bullying hysteria (some countries have actually passed national anti-bullying laws), it's small wonder to find all manner of overreaching. The current Miss America has decided world peace can wait: The eradication of bullying is much more important. In Ottawa, Canada, justice minister Martin Cauchon, confessing he'd been bullied as a kid for a family name that sounds like the French word for "pig," launched a multi-year anti-bullying campaign at a three-day conference entitled "Fear and Loathing—a symposium on bullying." The Canadian government supports about 100 anti-bullying projects, such as the one that uses positive role model "Buddy Beaver" to combat the nefarious "Punky" the skunk. So it is little surprise that Ontario Liberal leader Dalton McGuinty proposed $5 million worth of anti-bullying programs after his son was mugged—not in school, but on the way home from work.

In Edmonton, police asked the city council to enact bullying bylaws that would enable them to fine bullies up to $250—not just for stealing lunch money, but for "name-calling and intimidation." Here at home, down in New Orleans, school officials have begun levying fines against the parents of kids who fight at school. In Costa Mesa, California, a school district decided that not only was teasing possible grounds for expulsion, but even glaring at a classmate in a threatening manner might get a student bounced.

Parents are no longer teaching kids the fundamentals that used to get covered at home.

In Hastings, Minnesota, prosecutor James Backstrom decided that a student who picked a fight or harassed another would be punished with at least one night in jail (one female bully has been locked up 13 times). Now that the hurly-burly of the playground has actually been criminalized, it stands to reason that all sorts of boutique bullying complaints would emerge. These days, stories abound of "e-bullying," as well as "menace by mobile"—kids being bullied through messages left on their mobile phones (messages they're encouraged to save against the event of litigation).

Now pandemic, the anti-bullying movement is even extending to adults. Today, there are books like *The Bully at Work—What You Can Do to Stop the Hurt and Reclaim Your Dignity on the Job*. For years in Britain, some have been trying to pass a Dignity at Work bill, which defines bullying as "unjustified criticism on more than one occasion." *Computer Weekly* recently reported that one in five British computer geeks—or "IT professionals," if you prefer—claimed to have been bullied at work in the past year (including 17 percent of senior management).

A laughable program

Read enough of these stories—there are plenty more—and what a "reasonable person" might find offensive is not the prevalence of bullying, but the madness of those overcompensating to correct it in the anti-bullying movement. Which brings us back to Peter Yarrow's "Don't Laugh At Me" program. . . .

Color me cynical, but the temptation when listening to Peter Yarrow warble "Don't Laugh at Me" is, of course, to laugh at him. Just picturing literal-minded second-graders trying to get through the lyric "I'm fat, I'm thin, I'm short, I'm tall, I'm deaf, I'm blind, Hey aren't we all?" makes one titter. But to see if the song passes the laugh test, I run it by my own personal focus group on such matters—my 11-year-old niece.

She goes to a tony private school, and is accustomed to faddish character-education Nerf-speak. She tells me that the kids at her school are part of a "trustworthy community"—so trustworthy, in fact, that they're forbidden to put locks on their lockers. "My best friend Loren just had 20 bucks stolen," she says. When I play her the song, she doesn't get past the first line without erupting in laughter.

This hardly seems enough to go on, however. At the "Don't Laugh At Me" website, there are all sorts of student testimonials to the benefit of such programs. In one, a student writes, "What is hate? Hate is like jealous fish that don't talk to each other . . . Hate tastes like lemon, and it doesn't taste as good as honey. So, don't be jealous fish, let's be happy monkeys. In fact, let's be hatebusters."

A DLAM workshop

In order to get a better sense of the program and possibly transform myself from a jealous fish into a happy monkey—I head to Chippewa Falls, Wisconsin, for a "Don't Laugh At Me" (DLAM) workshop. On a freezing day, at the Cooperative Educational Services Agency, about 40 teachers, principals, and counselors pack into a multi-purpose room, their voices commingling in a pleasant 'Sconi-flavored hum of "you betcha's" and "Don'cha know's," as they discuss "dose Badgers" and the merits of the local Leinenkugel brewery's "Big Butt" Doppelbock.

Our facilitator, Sherrie Gammage, is from New Orleans, and works with Educators for Social Responsibility, who instruct teachers in all manner of trendy New Educationist theory, from conflict resolution to "emotional learning." Sherrie is a large African-American woman who describes herself as "abundant" (there's no large or small in a DLAM world). She holds out her hand by way of greeting, instructing, "Don't laugh at me." I try not to, but it's hard, since her own wheezing guffaw after every third comment makes me think of Smedley the cartoon dog.

Sherrie, whose students call her "Momma Sherrie," comes off . . . like the sassy neighbor on a UPN sitcom. She's squeezing two days of DLAM instruction into a single day, so she tells us not to panic. "Just sit back. Chill. Think of yourself as a pot roast marinating," she says.

"We're gonna have fun today, we're gonna laugh, we're gonna joke." As she says this, she cuts her hand on a piece of paper. A school nurse rushes to her aid, applying a Band-Aid. "I love to be taken care of by the mommies," she purrs. Sherrie uses our input to come up with classroom rules. We are allowed to "burp, sneeze, and cough because those are natural organic qualities." We can giggle. There are no tests. The only thing she asks of us is to "pay attention to what has heart and meaning for you," and to "speak your truth, but only as you feel safe enough to do it." She entrusts us with responsibility, because we are, she reminds us in the self-congratulatory language of the anti-bullying movement, not only adults, but "adults committed to a certain values and way of being. Take care of yourself."

[Bullying is] a teaching tool for kids. It teaches them how to get along with people.

Sherrie makes us watch a video featuring our maximum leader, Peter Yarrow. He brings us greetings, talking about the beauty of "peace education work" and the "heartfelt message of music" that can begin to launch us on "an extraordinary adventure, a pathway to doing something that might seem impossible." With all his world-of-wonder oiliness, he sounds like Willie Wonka without the good humor.

Sherrie gives us a bunch of scary statistics on school violence: One claims that 160,000 students skip school every day because of fear. (I later check the literature for purposes of comparison, but can find no study on how many stay home to watch *The View*.) Sherrie tells us the importance of defining bullying so we can combat it. While she allows there are many definitions, she settles on one from Olweus: "A person is being bullied . . . when he or she is exposed repeatedly and over time to negative actions on the part of one or more persons."

A class-participation exercise

Glad that's settled, we move on to one of oh-so-many class-participation exercises, some of which I evade more successfully than others. After showing an additional video of Yarrow singing the DLAM song to "put us in a place where we can get in touch with our feelings," Sherrie pairs us off to discuss our experiences of being bullied and how we dealt with them.

My partner is Mike Erickson, a bespectacled middleschool principal with an avuncular, honest face. . . . Sherrie tells us to be good listeners, to show empathy, to be conscious of "eye contact, of the way you hold your arms. Think of yourself as a vessel." I am still thinking of myself as a pot roast, but I manage the transition. I almost tell Mike about how I earned my seventh-grade nickname, "Crusty," but then think better of it. "It wouldn't put me in a safe place," I say. "Okay," he answers understandingly, making eye contact.

Instead, I tell him about how, in fourth grade, two classmates decided they'd jump me after school each day. I fended them off for a while, but I was outnumbered. So after four or five days of this, I used my "interpersonal skills," as the conflict resolutionists would say, and rallied the rest of the male population of the class to wait in ambush for my assailants. The next time they lunged at me, my friends rode in like the cavalry and beat the crap out of poor Michael Palmer and Michael Cassidy. They all ended up in the principal's office, while I made it unmolested to the bus. It wasn't my finest hour. But the Michaels never bothered me again.

Sherrie tells us it's now our partner's turn, and Erickson recounts his own travails with bullying. When he was in seventh grade, he says, an older kid would always throw him a sharp elbow as he got on the bus. Every day he dreaded it. Until one day, he came up with a solution: He slugged the bully in the face. "Then I jumped on top of him," he says, with barely contained relish. "Ya hear ya should never get in a fight," Erickson says, "but there comes a point . . ." I ask Erickson whether, as a principal, he ever gives that advice to his students—whether he ever tells them what parents have been telling their kids for ages: to stand up to a bully. "As a parent I might," he says, "but as a principal, I'd never tell them that." No doubt it would be a great way to get hit with a lawsuit. Still, Erickson is frustrated. "When kids come to me with harassment, it's difficult, because sometimes it doesn't help when I talk to a kid who's harassing another kid. . . . I don't have time to go through an eight-month program teaching them how not to harass kids."

Mike and other teachers throughout the day tell me parents are no longer teaching kids the fundamentals that used to get covered at home. It's not that the parents aren't teaching anything, the teachers grumble. They teach the kids how to be materialistic (most wouldn't even think of letting their kid's 16th birthday pass without getting them a car). They infuse their kids with loads of self-esteem ("They tell their kids they're better than everyone else," says one counselor). They teach them how to be oversexed, so that a gaggle of typical 12-year-old girls walking down the hall in their low-cut butt-cleavage-baring jeans looks like a gang of underfed plumbers.

What they often don't do, complain the teachers, is instill a sense of right and wrong, including the need to show kindness to others. Which is perhaps why we're stuck at an in-service with all this talk of safe spaces, using innocuously assertive "I" messages instead of more accusatory "you" messages. It's quite the balancing act. Especially, Mike whispers, since "what one person sees as harassment, the other says, 'Oh, he can't take a joke'—it's a gray area."

When we head back to the group and share our childhood bullying stories, I notice that a surprising number of successful anti-bullying interventions recollected by these mild-mannered Dairy State teachers end with the victim slugging the tormentor, never to be tormented again. During our "Connections" exercise, in which "we say anything we're thinking, feeling, or just any gifts you wanna give the group," I bring this up to Sherrie. She looks as if I've committed high heresy, and cautions that I only heard the stories people "felt safe enough to share."

This is a key tenet of the anti-bullying movement, whose theme song ought to be not "Don't Laugh At Me," but rather Morris Albert's '70s anthem "Feelings." That's what curricula like this are all about—nothing more than feelings. Knowing yourself. Revealing yourself. Feeling yourself. Even when the curriculum pays lip service to noble traits and actions (empathy, standing up for the weak, and so on), it buries them under so many layers of goo that the altruistic becomes the narcissistic. In the DLAM workshop and teacher's guides, feelings are highlighted in every single exercise. We play a "feelings pantomime," and take "feelings inventories" with 100-word-long lists of feelings—because, Sherrie says, children need to be able to express their feelings, especially "when their needs are not being met."

Think I'm exaggerating? A typical sentence from a curriculum guide boasts of supporting "the healthy expression of feelings in young people, including how to build a feelings vocabulary, encourage discussion about feelings, reflect back young people's moods, support young people's empathy, infuse feelings reflection across the curriculum, and much more."

Role-playing games have names like "Emotion Motions," "How Would You Feel If . . ." and "The Feelings Echo," in which students complete the sentence, "I feel cared for when . . ." When they are asked to "play mirrors" with another child, they concentrate not on the other person, but on what it feels like "to mirror someone." Kids are instructed to use "journaling" to help them "explore feelings." They are told "all feelings are important," and they are to "brainstorm about how to share what they've learned about feelings with the rest of the school." Ultimately, after signing off on their "Constitution of Caring" (and after closing out the day's session with the recommended rendition of "If I Had a Hammer"), they are encouraged to share their "achievement" with outside officials like the President of the United States, as if he really needs to be bothered because Caitlin is proud of herself for writing in her feelings journal.

In the name of discouraging bullying and fostering empathy, students are told to "use class meetings to talk about feelings," to say "one word that describes how they are feeling that day." Their teachers, after they affirm that "crying is okay—regardless of our age or gender," are to "infuse feelings into [the] curriculum"—for instance, by discussing how figures from history felt about events of their day. At camps using the DLAM program, cabins are to "challenge one another to a game of 'Name that Feelings Tune'" (in which campers compete to "name as many songs as possible that include words expressing feelings").

DLAM in practice

By now, I admit, I am feeling downright skeptical. To make sure I'm not shortchanging the DLAM program, I go the next day to see it in practice. A school counselor I've met at the workshop, Tah Kempf, allows me to sit in on her DLAM instruction of a group of students at an intermediate school in Eleva, Wisconsin. A spunky, gifted communicator who exhibits total control over a couple of fifth-grade classes, Kempf is hardly the hippie-dippy, peace-and-love type. When I tell her that I'd really like to see her force her fifth-graders to sing "Puff the Magic Dragon" as the curriculum suggests, she rolls her eyes conspiratorially. "I don't think I can get them to do that," she says.

The rest of the way, however, she goes by the book. She tells the kids, with straight-faced understatement, that "this program talks a lot about feelings." She has them close their eyes, then plays the DLAM song. She employs reverse psychology when a good number of kids start giggling. "Sometimes we laugh when something is really close to our hearts," she says. "So don't judge each other if you hear someone laughing." She has the kids sit in a circle on the floor beneath posters proclaiming positive messages like "101 Ways to Praise a Child." A Koosh-ball is thrown to a child, indicating it's his turn to speak. One or two catch it in the face, but that doesn't stop the kids from completing the exercise with gusto. Their task is to mention as many put-downs as they can.

They quickly warm to it. There's all the usual fare. A mousy, hesitant kid with frames as big as his head says, "Some people will call you four eyes." A girl says the tomboys in the class make fun of her for wearing pink. When I interview kids on the side, one tells me he gets called "roly poly oly because I'm fat." Another with a chapped ring around his mouth tells me, "I have a licking problem, and some people call me Licker Lips."

DLAM instructors like to say that there are no wrong answers. And that becomes apparent as the minutes drag like hours. At first sensitized to the whole world of slights that have been directed at them, the kids gradually drift away from actual ridicule and shoot off in every direction. One girl says she is teased for liking somebody. A white teacher joins the fun, and says reverse discrimination against white people is a problem, "even though everyone around this area is very white." A boy says that a good example of a put-down is "maybe when you go to the waterpark, and when you get there, there's not a lot to go on."

"Ohhh, disappointment, yeahhh," seconds Tali.

After the session, I grab seven kids (four girls and three boys), and ask them questions. They seem fairly confused by this turn of events. When asked how many of them consider themselves bullies, all seven say they are. When asked how many of them consider themselves bullying victims, all seven are just as convinced. I'm put in mind of something my wife, herself a former first grade teacher, told me after she taught a required lesson on "inappropriate touch." The next day, little Tyler could not remove a piece of lint from little Ashley's sweater without being accused of "inappropriately touching" her.

Little evidence of success

Despite the drawbacks, anti-bullying programs like these might still have some value if they did what they purported to do. But there's not much evidence of that, and some to the contrary. Bergen University's Dan Olweus, for instance, claims that after his anti-bullying program (which is less touchy-feely than DLAM) was implemented, instances of bullying declined 50 percent or more over a two-year period. But other anti-bullying researchers say those numbers have not been replicated. Olweus himself has lamented the elusiveness of much anti-bullying work, citing a study that found just 10 violence-prevention programs out of 400 met any specified minimum criteria for evaluation.

Likewise, while much anti-bullying research reads like propaganda, two clear-eyed studies by a couple of Australian professors—who generally support anti-bullying programs—have shed greater light on the discipline. Ken Rigby, of the University of South Australia, examined 13 studies of the effectiveness of anti-bullying curricula from around the world. Of those, 12 found at least slight decreases in some kinds of bullying. But 7 reported simultaneous increases in other kinds of bullying. The University of Western Sydney's Robert Parada reached an even bleaker conclusion. His two-year study, believed to be the largest of its kind, surveyed 4,500 high school students who'd participated in anti-bullying programs. He found that the level of bullying they experienced, despite all the peer support, mediation, and self-esteem-building, "remained exactly the same" as ten years before, he told the *Sydney Morning Herald*, the only change being the new political pressure to say it wasn't.

What is impossible to quantify, however, is the deeper effect of trying to eradicate all bullying. Richard Hazler, a professor of counselor education at Ohio University, who has taught seminars on curbing bullying, says, "There's a normalcy in this whole process. I don't want to say that bullying is okay. But it's a teaching tool for kids. It teaches them to get along with people, how to use power, the victims—how to obtain power when not in power positions. How do we stop bullying and victimization? I hate to make this case in public. But we don't entirely want to—because if kids didn't have it—how would they learn? These are mistakes they're making. We want a cooperative atmosphere, but we also want to show them how to deal with aggression."

"Grief stricken, heartbroken, and helpless"

Back in the fifth-grade classroom, Tali winds things up. After a 25-minute discussion of putdowns, we are in touch with our feelings. I know I am with mine. Glancing down the "Don't Laugh At Me Feelings Inventory," I quietly reflect I am being made "afraid, anxious, and exasperated" by what we are doing to these kids. I am "horrified, nervous, and paranoid" that we are not teaching them resilience, but rather, turning them into human flypaper. Every insult—even ones formerly sloughed off—now sticks, and gets reclassified and inflated, as children are encouraged to nurse the memory of petty hurts. I feel "sad, sorrowful, and suspicious" that we are teaching them to be nervous nellies and lunchroom litigators. That we are teaching them to feel "persecuted, self-pitying" and pusillanimous—the last of which is not on my feelings inventory but is a feeling I nonetheless feel entitled to express.

The whole thing makes me "contemptuous, crabby, and cruel." Until what happens next. As Tali concludes the class by once again playing Peter Yarrow's "Don't Laugh At Me," I hear a fifth-grader say as he exits the room, "What an awesome song!" I have a revelation—that things are much worse than I believed. I feel "grief stricken, heartbroken, and helpless." For I now see it clearly: We are raising something much more depressing than the wussified children I've just described.

We are raising the next generation of Peter, Paul & Mary fans.

3

Zero-Tolerance Policies Are Necessary to Prevent School Violence

Kay S. Hymowitz

Kay S. Hymowitz is a senior fellow at the Manhattan Institute, a New York–based public policy research organization, and a contributing editor for City Journal. *She writes extensively on education and childhood in America and is the author of* Ready or Not: Why Treating Children as Small Adults Endangers Their Future and Ours.

Zero-tolerance polices have been criticized for resulting in severe penalties for seemingly minor offenses, such as offhand comments about violence, violent drawings, or playful simulations of violent acts. However, the policies have headed off potentially catastrophic shootings and bombings nationwide. Because it is impossible to discern a teenager's true intentions, any hint of potential violence must be taken seriously in order to protect the safety of other students.

Editor's Note: Zero-tolerance policies impose strict penalties—usually suspension or expulsion—on students who bring weapons to school or make any threat of violence, however innocuous it may seem.

The recent arrest of two 8-year-old Irvington, N.J., boys accused of making "terroristic threats" for pointing paper guns at their classmates have led many people to add "zero tolerance" to the list of things that the schools can't get right. A wave of these kinds of suspensions and arrests seems all the clumsier since, as experts are quick to remind us, the numbers show that school violence is on the wane.

Yet while events during the past month since 15-year-old Charles "Andy" Williams killed two classmates and wounded 13 other people in a shooting spree at Santana High School in Santee, Calif., may not justify arresting 8-year-olds playing "bang-bang you're dead," they do suggest

Kay S. Hymowitz, "Zero Tolerance Is Schools' First Line of Defense," *Newsday*, April 18, 2001, p. A31. Copyright © 2001 by Tribune Media Services, Inc. All rights reserved. Reproduced by permission.

that the decline in school violence may have more to do with students being quicker to report suspicious classmates and authorities taking those reports seriously than any lack of budding Klebolds and Harrises, the Columbine High School killers. In Santana's aftermath, a raft of students in communities ranging from New Canaan, Conn., to inner-city Houston threatened to follow Williams.

It's not so easy to distinguish the prankster from the wild-eyed adolescent with a plan when lives are at stake.

Sure, some of these kids, like the New Jersey boys, were harmless playground jokesters and braggarts. But it's not so easy to distinguish the prankster from the wild-eyed adolescent with a plan when lives are at stake. Last week in a San Antonio high school, two vice principals received e-mails saying, "Watch the Sniper. You'll never know when we'll get you. We're coming behind you. You'll never know when the bullet hits."

The 18-year-old accused of sending the e-mails insisted they were a "joke." Should authorities believe him? The day before Andy Williams killed two classmates, he had reassured friends he was only joking about pulling a Columbine.

In a staggering number of cases over this month, students appear to have been deadly serious. Right after the Santana shooting, at Twenty-nine Palms, Calif.—where Andy Williams lived until moving to Santee six months before the shooting—police nabbed two high school kids with a .22-caliber rifle and a hit list. And in El Cajon, Calif., just seven miles from Santee, an 18-year-old loner known as "the Rock" for his intimidating physique nearly succeeded in killing some of his classmates, opening fire with a shotgun in his high school, wounding three students and two teachers before police stopped him.

And the mayhem has continued. In the last few weeks, threats disrupted schools in Charlotte, Cincinnati, Newport News, Providence, Milwaukee, Minneapolis, Louisville, several California counties and Omaha. Bomb threats closed schools in Westfield Township, Ohio, and close to home in Nyack in Rockland County, and Greenburgh, Harrison and Armonk in Westchester. On Long Island, officials in Roosevelt cancelled classes for two days earlier this month when a combination of fights, false fire alarms and bomb threats had rocked the town's junior-senior high school.

Administrators cannot comfort themselves by chalking these post-Santana incidents up to copy-cat behavior. There were five near-misses in the six weeks before Santana, none of which received national press coverage at the time. In those cases, the potential for carnage was huge: Police discovered guns, bombs, hit lists and school floor plans in the homes of the student suspects in Elmira, N.Y.; Palm Harbor, Fla.; Fort Collins, Col.; Hoyt, Kansas; and Cupertino, Calif.

From the point of view of teachers, administrators are hardly the zealous disciplinarians that some reports suggest. One study from the Texas Public Policy Foundation showed that nearly two-thirds of Texas public

SHELBYVILLE-SHELBY COUNTY
PUBLIC LIBRARY

school teachers thought that teacher morale was worsening in their schools, and 40 percent of them cited "student attitudes and behavior" and administrative failure to address them as the principal reasons. "There are no serious consequences for bad behavior, vulgar language or rude treatment of teachers by students," one teacher lamented. "The students run our school," another wrote. In Boston, after a rash of attacks on teachers this year, the teachers' union did a survey showing that 58 percent of high school teachers and 40 percent of middle school teachers were dissatisfied with administrators' efforts to control school discipline.

And the problem is likely to get worse. The Connecticut Department of Education released a summary of disciplinary offenses in its public schools that included 2,000 or so first-graders, kindergartners and even preschoolers. More zero-tolerance policies run amok? It doesn't seem like it. Jeanne Milstein, child advocate for the State of Connecticut, says that her office had received many reports about "out of control" tots hitting, biting and throwing things in inner-city and suburban schools. Though there's little solid data, Kristie Kauerz, an official at the Education Commission of the States, claims that there's enough anecdotal evidence to conclude that a growing number of unmanageable babes is now a nationwide trend.

In the end, zero tolerance may be more symptom than cure for the uneasy disciplinary climate of our schools. Certainly it's no final answer to out-of-control 5-year-olds or revenge-crazed teenagers. But as the threats continue and the bombs and guns appear, it's all we've got.

4

Zero-Tolerance Policies Are Absurd

John Derbyshire

John Derbyshire is a literary critic, commentator, and novelist who lives in New York. He is a columnist and a contributing editor for the National Review, *a conservative weekly journal.*

Zero-tolerance policies require school administrators to impose harsh penalties on students who bring weapons to school or who threaten violence. These policies have resulted in students' receiving ridiculously severe punishments for minor infractions. Schools' reliance on the zero-tolerance approach reveals the detrimental influence of liberal ideology on American society: School administrators, seeped in liberal values, cannot be trusted to use sound judgment regarding school discipline; therefore, an inflexible policy has been created to substitute for common sense. Instead of relying on a rigid, bureaucratic policy like zero tolerance, schools must impart moral values, good manners, and respect for authority while punishing only those few students who genuinely behave inappropriately.

You know the stories. They have been cropping up in everyday conversation among all classes and conditions of Americans for four or five years now.

• A Pittsburgh kindergartner was disciplined in 1998 because his Halloween firefighter costume included a plastic axe.

• A ten-year-old girl at McElwain Elementary in Thornton, Colo., repeatedly asked a certain boy on the playground if he liked her. The boy complained to a teacher. School administrators threatened to suspend the girl, citing the school's "zero tolerance" guidelines for sexual harassment.

• In Cobb County, Ga., a sixth-grader was suspended because the ten-inch key chain on her Tweety Bird wallet was considered a weapon in violation of the school's zero-tolerance policy.

• In November 1997, a Colorado Springs school district suspended six-year-old Seamus Morris under the school's zero-tolerance drug policy.

John Derbyshire, "The Problem with 'Zero': On Tolerance and Common Sense in the Schools," *National Review*, vol. 53, May 28, 2001. Copyright © 2001 by National Review, Inc., 215 Lexington Ave., New York, NY 10016. Reproduced by permission.

The drug? Organic lemon drops from a health-food store.

• T.J. West, aged 13, drew a picture of a Confederate flag on a scrap of paper. His school in Derby, Kan., had listed the flag as a "hate" symbol, so West was suspended for racial harassment and intimidation. This one went to federal court. The boy lost, took his case to the Tenth U.S Circuit Court of Appeals, lost again, and took it to the U.S. Supreme Court, which refused to hear it.

It would be comforting to think that all this "zero tolerance" insanity was driven by dimwitted administrators and avaricious lawyers. No doubt some of it is, but in at least one recent case in New York City, zero tolerance has been enforced by parents. A ten-year-old boy at a Brooklyn public school was taunted for being overweight and Jewish. At last he threatened to bring his dad's gun to school. The boy was transferred to a different school and charged with juvenile harassment. When parents at his new school got wind of the incident, hundreds of them pulled their kids from classes in protest. The boy's father did indeed have a handgun—legally owned and registered, kept in a combination-lock safe bolted to the floor. Police took the gun away. The boy is now being homeschooled.

Inflexible application of bureaucratic rules

For some insight into a professional educator's point of view, I spoke to the principal of my own children's elementary school. Suppose, I put it to him, my son were to say, in the course of a schoolyard dispute: "I'll get my dad's gun and shoot you." Would I then be facing the arrest of my son and the seizure of my property? The principal laughed. "Certainly not. We all know each other here. I know your kids, I know you. If necessary I'd call you in for a chat. Stuff like that happens in big schools where kids are anonymous and staff turnover is high. They should be dealt with informally. But you can only do that when the informal relationships have been built up."

No doubt that is much easier to say when you are principal of an elementary school rather than a high school. The principal of my local high school would not talk to me about zero tolerance, handing me up to the district superintendent of schools—a sensible man who said he thought these policies were becoming less popular, and that he personally supported absolute zero tolerance only in matters of gang membership, a growing problem even in quiet suburban communities such as ours. If it is true that zero tolerance is beginning to decline, that is good news. No human institution can be run by the inflexible application of bureaucratic rules, without any regard for individual cases or any attempt on the part of those in authority to apply thoughtful judgment to situations. Why would anybody think it could?

A response to liberal follies

Popular support for zero-tolerance laws and rules is in large part a reaction to the follies of our liberal elites. Why do citizens want rigid, mandatory, bureaucratic rules for dealing with transgressions? For the same reason we want three-strikes laws and capital punishment: because we have learned that if we rely on soft-headed ideological judges, parole boards, and school administrators to do the right thing, we will be disappointed. The results delivered by zero-tolerance rules may sometimes be wacky; the results delivered when our liberal elites are left free to exercise their powers of judgment are positively dangerous. Zero tolerance is one more response to the moral crisis of our time: to the collapse of authority, to the turning away from customary and traditional practices and beliefs, to moral relativism and its *tout comprendre c'est tout pardonner* attitude to crime; to all the furrowed-brow, equivocating, guilt-addled, apologetic dross of modern liberalism.

No human institution can be run by the inflexible application of bureaucratic rules, without any regard for individual cases.

This being America, there is also the matter of race, with all the associated rancor and delusions. Zero-tolerance policies in schools came about partly because the schools faced lawsuits charging that principals disciplined students unequally based on race and other factors. In this regard, the subsequent results have been dismally predictable: By the late 1990s, with zero tolerance well entrenched in schools nationwide, complaints were being heard that these boilerplate, inflexible policies also led to discrimination! By 1997, the nation's schools were blanketed with zero-tolerance policies; yet, in the 1997–98 academic year, of the roughly 87,000 students expelled from their schools, about 31 percent were black, even though blacks make up only 17 percent of enrollment. Tony Arasi, assistant schools superintendent in Cobb County, Ga., made this point in commenting on the Tweety Bird case: "Those people saying zero tolerance leads to unfairness . . . may want to go back 10 or 15 years to before most districts had zero tolerance. They were saying there was unfairness then. It's come full circle."

The abdication of authority

The paradox is that zero tolerance of threats, drugs, weapons, and "sexual harassment" coexists with 100 percent tolerance of "lifestyles" that most emphatically would not have been tolerated thirty years ago, and that very large numbers of Americans still find offensive. Following the April 1999 Columbine school shootings in Littleton, Colo., it emerged that students at the school had worn Nazi emblems and given Hitler salutes to each other in the hallways, without any disciplinary sanction. (Colorado was, by the way, a leader in zero-tolerance school policies long before the Columbine massacre.) And of course, every kind of sexual activity is now a "lifestyle choice" that adolescents are perfectly free to make without interference from authority. The abdication of authority is, in fact, the common feature underlying both zero tolerance and total tolerance. On the one hand, there is the determination to avoid exercising any kind of rational leniency about petty infractions of discipline, lest one's judgment betray one into "discrimination" or—much worse—fail to detect the very occasional adolescent psychopath. On the other hand, there is the unwillingness to be "judgmental" about any expressions of individual belief or taste—except those derived from organized Christianity.

A child's chance of being shot dead in school is around one in a million, which is to say about one-third his risk of being struck by lightning.

And those school shootings—Pearl, Miss., and West Paducah, Ky., in 1997; Jonesboro, Ark., Edenboro, Pa., and Springfield, Ore., in 1998; Littleton, Colo., in 1999; Santee, Calif., and El Cajon, Calif., in March 2001—are engraved on the mind of every school administrator in the country, and on the minds of most parents too. The Santee shooting was on a Monday, and the 15-year-old boy who did it spent all weekend telling friends about his intention. Nobody took him seriously. You see the point of those Brooklyn parents pulling their kids from school. It is of very little use to say to these parents that a child's chance of being shot dead in school is around one in a million, which is to say about one-third his risk of being struck by lightning; nor does it help to point out that schools have never been perfectly safe from violence, and that the idea of taking a gun to your teachers and classmates did not emerge suddenly into the world in 1997. The worst school massacre in U.S. history occurred in 1927, and the original shoot-up-the-school movie was Lindsay Anderson's *If. . .* , which was released in 1969 (and was itself inspired by Jean Vigo's 1933 movie *Zero for Conduct*).

Balancing *li* and *fa*

The bureaucratic inflexibility of zero-tolerance policies is one symptom of a more general problem our hedonistic, atomized society faces. To get some perspective, it may help to glance back for a moment across a couple of thousand years' time and ten thousand miles of space.

The two most potent philosophies of statecraft in ancient China were Confucianism and Legalism. The Confucians believed that human beings were fundamentally good, and that society could be regulated by internalized moral rules. Good manners, clear conscience, moral leadership, and a respect for customary ways of doing things—concepts wrapped up in the word *li*—would guarantee social order, according to the Confucians. The Legalists, in contrast, believed that human selfishness was too strong a force to be contained by anything but the fear of strict laws and savage punishments, rigorously and impartially applied. Only the firm, inflexible application of written law, *fa*, would keep society stable.

Any actual society, of course, needs some measure of both *li* and *fa*. Some of us are beyond the reach of moral precepts and can be held back from evil only by the threat of punishment. There are not many of this kind, though, as [eighteenth-century Scottish poet] Robert Burns pointed out to his young friend:

> I'll no[t] say, men are villains a[ll]:
> The real, harden'd wicked,
> Wha[t] ha[v]e nae check but human law,
> Are to a few restric[t]ed . . .

Most of us can be kept on the straight and narrow by some basic moral training in childhood, reinforced by the example of virtuous men and women in positions of authority and by the reassurance offered by traditional observances—that is, by good manners.

What the zero-tolerance follies tell us is that we have lost the balance between *li* and *fa*. We have slipped into Legalism, the application of inflexible, pettifogging punitive codes to all social infractions without judgment or wise consideration. To restore the balance, we need some wider appreciation of Confucius's insight—which has been shared by all great ethical and religious teachers—that human beings are, in the main, decent enough to respond to moral training and example, when those set in authority over them have the courage and conviction to supply those things. With a little more *li* in our lives, we should be less oppressed by *fa*. How we get from here to there is, of course, another question.

5

Increased Security Measures Can Help Prevent School Violence

Mary W. Green

Mary W. Green is a security specialist at the School Security Technologies and Resource Center at Sandia National Laboratories, a government agency that develops technologies for national security.

Various security devices and policies can be implemented in schools to deter and prevent violent behavior. Technologies such as cameras, metal detectors, and locks on exterior doors can help administrators keep weapons off campus and monitor students' actions, while policies including mandatory uniforms and random searches provide additional security. These measures cannot completely guarantee that violence will not occur, but they can reduce students' opportunities to commit violence while increasing the likelihood of them being caught.

M ost schools in the United States are safe institutions, with disciplinary issues creating most disruptions. However, because of the 1998 campus slayings involving students, firearms, and multiple victims, schools and school programs are working harder to reach out to students, to teach them to be good citizens, to identify potentially dangerous personalities, and to develop appropriate intervention strategies. There are many excellent programs around the country that address the issues of bullying, anger, hate, abuse, drugs, alcohol, gangs, lack of role models, vandalism, and so forth. It is of great importance to the United States that these programs be pursued expeditiously. Unfortunately, these programs cannot be successful overnight (indeed, many must be initiated early in a child's life in order to be most effective) and do not yet exist in all schools. Meanwhile, security incidents are occurring in schools that must be dealt with now—perpetrators must be caught and consequences must be administered. School administrators would like to discourage security infractions by means of any deterrent available to them. One such ap-

Mary W. Green, *The Appropriate and Effective Use of Security Technologies in U.S. Schools: A Guide for Schools and Law Enforcement Agencies.* Washington, DC: National Institute of Justice, 1999.

proach sought more often today involves security technologies.

Security technologies are not the answer to all school security problems. However, many security products (e.g., cameras, sensors, and so forth) can be excellent tools if applied appropriately. They can provide school administrators or security officials with information that would not otherwise be available, free up manpower for more appropriate work, or be used to perform mundane tasks. Sometimes they can save a school money (compared to the long-term cost of personnel or the cost impact of not preventing a particular incident). Too often, though, these technologies are not applied appropriately in schools, are expected to do more than they are capable of, or are not well maintained after initial installation. In these cases, technologies are certainly not cost effective.

Why security technologies?

To reduce problems of crime or violence in schools: (1) the opportunities for security infractions should be eliminated or made more difficult to accomplish, (2) the likelihood of being caught must be greatly increased, and (3) consequences must be established and enforced. Item 3 is a social and political issue and needs to be addressed head on by school boards and communities across the country. This guide addresses only items 1 and 2.

Many security products (e.g., cameras, sensors, and so forth) can be excellent tools if applied appropriately.

Simply providing more adults, especially parents, in schools will reduce the opportunities for security infractions and increase the likelihood of being caught. However, adding dedicated professional security staff to perform very routine security functions has many limitations:

- Locating qualified people may be difficult.
- Humans do not do mundane tasks well.
- Manpower costs are always increasing.
- Turnover of security personnel can be detrimental to a security program.
- As in other security environments, more repetitious tasks become boring.

Hence, the possible role of security technologies expands. Through technology, a school can introduce ways to collect information or enforce procedures and rules that it would not be able to afford or rely on security personnel to do.

Why security technologies have not been embraced

Anyone working in the security field is aware that there are thousands of security products on the market. Some of them are excellent, but many claim to be "the very best of its kind." And, unfortunately, there are a significant number of customers in the country who have been less than pleased with the ultimate cost, maintenance requirements, and effectiveness of security technologies they have purchased. Schools have been no exception to this and have a few inherent problems of their own:

- Schools do not usually have the funding for aggressive and complete security programs.
- Schools generally lack the ability to procure effective security technology products and services at the lowest bid.
- Many school security programs cannot afford to hire well-trained security personnel.
- School administrators and their staff rarely have training or experience in security technologies.
- Schools have no infrastructures in place for maintaining or upgrading security devices—when something breaks, it is often difficult to have it repaired or replaced.
- Issues of privacy and potential civil rights lawsuits may prohibit or complicate the use of some technologies.

Arguments often used against security initiatives:	Some counter-arguments:
• "We've never done it that way before."	• "We need to evolve our security strategies to keep up with the changing times."
• "This is a knee-jerk reaction."	• "This solution will take care of the immediate threat while longer term social programs are put into place."
• "Our school will look like a prison."	• "Our school will look like it is well controlled."
• "Students' rights may be infringed upon."	• "Students have a right to a safe and secure school environment."
• "People will think we have a bad school."	• "We will gain a reputation for controlling our problems."
• "We may be sued."	• "We may be sued if we don't take this action."

The issues come down to applying security technologies in schools that are effective, affordable, and politically acceptable but still useful within these difficult constraints.

Effectiveness, affordability, and acceptability

Effectiveness, affordability, and acceptability are difficult tradeoffs and, occasionally, a seemingly ineffective solution to a security problem is chosen because of a lack of funding or pressure from the community to do something.

Although many effective security measures are too expensive for schools, cost alone is not often the ultimate driver. Most major changes to security policies, including the introduction of technologies, are often brought on not by foresight but as a response to some undesirable incident.

This is not to say that a good argument should be made for applying every physical security approach in every school. "Appropriate" preparation is, by far, the greater "art" in security system design, and it includes an evolving plan, beginning with defining a particular school's risks. . . .

Identifying the security risks at a school

In the past, schools have rarely understood the need or had the time or resources to consider their security plans from a systems perspective—looking at the big picture of what they are trying to achieve in order to arrive at the optimal security strategy. A school's security staff must understand what it is trying to protect (people and/or high-value assets), who it is trying to protect against (the threats), and the general environment and constraints that it must work within—the characterization of the facility. This understanding will allow a school to define its greatest and/or most likely risks so that its security strategy consciously addresses those risks. This strategy will likely include some combination of technologies, personnel, and procedures that do the best possible job of solving the school's problems within its financial, logistical, and political constraints.

Why is this careful identification of risk important? Because few facilities, especially schools, can afford a security program that protects against all possible incidents.

No two schools are alike and, therefore, there is no single approach to security that will work ideally for all schools. From year to year, even, a school's security strategy will need revision because the world around it and the people inside it will always be changing.

Major changes to security policies . . . are often brought on not by foresight but as a response to some undesirable incident.

Defining a school's assets. For this school year, what is most at risk? The protection of the students and staff is always at the top of this list, but the measures taken to protect them will usually be driven by the defined threats. Are the instruments in the band hall very attractive targets for theft or vandalism? Is the new computer lab full of the best and most easily resold computers? Though desirable, a school cannot possibly afford to protect everything to the same level of confidence.

Defining a school's threats. For this school year, who or what is your school threatened by? Gang rivalries? Fights behind the gym? Drugs hidden in lockers? Guns brought to school? Outsiders on campus? Drinking at lunchtime? Vehicle breakins? Graffiti in the bathrooms? Accidents in the parking lot? How sophisticated (knowledgeable of their task of malevolence) or motivated (willing to risk being caught or injured) do the perpetrators seem to be? Measures taken to protect against these threats are driven by the characterization of the facility and its surroundings as mentioned earlier.

Characterizing school's environment. Any security strategy must incorporate the counts of the facility so that all strengths, weaknesses, and idiosyncrasies are realized and provided for. How risks are approached will largely be driven by facility constraints. If theft and vandalism are primary risks for your school, answers to questions regarding the physical plant will determine the optimal security measures. Is the school new or old? Are the windows particularly vulnerable? Does everyone who ever worked at the school still have keys? What is the nighttime lighting like? Does the interior intrusion sensor system work well, or do the local police ignore the alarms due to a high false-alarm rate? Are visitors forced or merely requested to go through the front office before accessing the rest of the school?

If issues of violence are a major concern, a thorough understanding of employees, student profiles, and neighborhood characteristics will be necessary.

If outsiders on campus are a primary concern, it will be necessary to recognize the facility's ability to control unauthorized access. How many entry points are there into the buildings? Are gangs present in the area? Are the school grounds open and accessible to anyone, or do fences or buildings restrict access? Is there easy access to the school roof? Where are hiding places within the building or on the premises? Is the student population small enough so that most of the staff would recognize most of the students and parents?

If issues of violence are a major concern, a thorough understanding of employees, student profiles, and neighborhood characteristics will be necessary. What is the crime rate in the neighborhood? Is the school administration well liked by the students? Are teachers allowed access to the school at night? Are students allowed off campus at lunch time? How much spending money do students generally have? Are popular hangouts for young people close by and, for business establishments, does management collaborate with the school? Are expelled or suspended students sent home or to an alternative school? How many incidents of violence have occurred at the school over the past 4 years? What is the general reputation of the school, and how does it appear to an outsider? Are your most vocal parents prosecurity or proprivacy? Do your students like and respect your security personnel well enough to pass them pieces of information regarding security concerns? Once the school's threats, assets, and environmental constraints are understood, the security needs can be prioritized such that the school's security goals are understood by all those involved. . . .

Designing the school security system

After identifying the risks or concerns at a noneducational facility, a methodical approach to the security plan would then examine possible solutions to each area of vulnerability from the perspective of:

Detection → Delay → Response

For any problem, it is necessary first to detect that an incident or problem is occurring. For example, when someone is breaking into a building, it is necessary that this act be detected and that information be supplied to the authorities as soon as possible. Next, this adversary must be delayed as long as possible so that the response force may arrive. A simple example of delay would be firmly bolting computer components onto large heavy desks, so that a thief is forced to use more time removing the bolts. Finally, someone, such as the police, must respond to the incident to catch the thief redhanded.

For a school environment, it is probably more appropriate to expand this model:

Deterrence → Detection → Delay → Response/
Investigation → Consequences

The most appealing step in any school security system should be to convince the perpetrator that he or she should not do whatever it is he or she is considering, whether the action is perceived as too difficult, not worthwhile, or the chances of being caught are quite high. Clearly, most security measures employed in facilities are intended for the precise purpose of deterrence, whether it be to discourage a thief, a drug dealer, or an errant employee. . . .

If a school is perceived as unsafe . . . , then "undesirables" will come in, and the school will actually become unsafe.

Unlike other facilities, where a perpetrator would be handed over to the authorities, and the consequences determined by law, a school often has the authority and/or opportunity to establish the consequences for incidents that occur on their campus. It is imperative, however, that schools do not assume authority that they do not have. Issues governed by law must be reported to the appropriate authority. . . .

A spectrum of physical security approaches

It will be assumed that consequences for undesirable actions have been put into place at a school; otherwise, there is little or no deterrence to be gained from any physical security measures designed to detect, delay, and respond to an incident. A wide array of security measures involving people, campus modifications, and/or technologies can be considered for most concerns, keeping in mind the unique characteristics of each school. A recurring message from school administrators is that the majority of their problems are brought onto campus by outsiders or expelled/suspended students so measures to keep outsiders off campus will generally be of global benefit. (Although this is not the case in all incidents, school administrators quite often find it more palatable to parents if security measures are justified based on the exterior threat rather than the suspicion of their children.) The following is a partial list of possible security measures to address various security issues:

(Most of the following suggested security measures are in use in one or more U.S. schools, but a few may not yet have been attempted. In any case, there is no comprehensive body of knowledge regarding their effectiveness. More research is needed to get a national picture on particular technologies. Also keep in mind that a school should always contact its legal counsel before participating in any new security program that involves searching or testing of people or property.)

Outsiders on campus
- Posted signs regarding penalties for trespassing.
- Enclosed campus (fencing).
- Guard at main entry gate to campus.
- Greeters in strategic locations.
- Student I.D.s or badges.
- Vehicle parking stickers.
- Uniforms or dress codes.
- Exterior doors locked from the outside.
- A challenge procedure for anyone out of class.
- Cameras in remote locations.
- School laid out so all visitors must pass through front office.
- Temporary "fading" badges issued to all visitors.

Fights on campus
- Cameras.
- Duress alarms.
- Whistles. . . .

Weapons
- Walk-through metal detectors.
- Hand-held metal detectors.
- Vapor detection of gun powder.
- Crimestopper hotline with rewards for information.
- Gunpowder detection swipes.
- Random locker, backpack, and vehicle searches.
- X-ray inspection of bookbags and purses.

Malicious acts
- Setback of all school buildings from vehicle areas.
- Inaccessibility of air intake and water source.
- All adults on campus required to have a badge.
- Vehicle barriers near main entries and student gathering areas.

Parking lot problems
- Cameras.
- Parking decals.
- Fencing.
- Card I.D. systems for parking lot entry.
- Parking lots sectioned off for different student schedules.
- Sensors in parking areas that should have no access during school-day.
- Roving guards.
- Bike patrol. . . .

Bomb threats
- Caller I.D. on phone system.
- Crimestopper program with big rewards for information.
- Recording all phone calls, with a message regarding this at the beginning of each incoming call.
- All incoming calls routed through a district office.
- Phone company support.

- No pay phones on campus.
- Policy to extend the school year when plagued with bomb threats and subsequent evacuations. . . .

Teacher safety
- Duress alarms.
- Roving patrols.
- Classroom doors left open during class.
- Cameras in black boxes in classrooms.
- Controlled access to classroom areas.

The role of order maintenance

One additional consideration that cannot be overlooked is the perception of a lack of order on a school campus. If a school is perceived as unsafe (i.e., it appears that no adult authority prevails on a campus), then "undesirables" will come in, and the school will actually become unsafe. This is an embodiment of the broken window theory: one broken window left unrepaired will encourage additional windows to be broken. Seemingly small incidents or issues such as litter on a school campus can provide the groundwork for (or even just the reputation of) a problem school. Issues of vandalism and theft can be almost as harmful to a school as actual violence because they can create a fertile environment for loss of control and community confidence.

Issues contributing to a school's overall order maintenance must therefore be taken seriously, not unlike any other public facility. Reducing theft, deterring vandalism and graffiti, keeping outsiders off campus, keeping the facility in good repair, improving poor lighting, maintaining attractive landscaping, and getting rid of trash are all important to school security.

Technologies such as cameras, sensors, microdots (for identifying ownership), and antigraffiti sealers can contribute significantly in many (but not all) situations and are possible approaches to further support a school's order maintenance.

6

Increased School Security Measures Violate Students' Rights

Randall R. Beger

Randall R. Beger is an associate professor in the Department of Sociology at the University of Wisconsin in Eau Claire and coordinator of the university's criminal justice program.

Despite the fact that schools are safe and that school violence is decreasing, school administrators have instituted extreme security measures, some involving devices such as cameras, metal detectors, and locks. In addition, the presence of law enforcement personnel on campuses has increased dramatically, and students are routinely subjected to undercover sting operations and surprise searches, some of which include the use of drug-sniffing dogs. These measures violate students' dignity as well as their constitutional right to due process and freedom from unreasonable searches and seizures. Students face a greater risk from the erosion of their constitutional rights than from the threat of violence.

> Look inside a high school, and you are looking in a mirror, under bright lights. How we treat our children, what they see and learn from us, tell us what is healthy and what is sick—and more about who we are than we may want to know.
> —Nancy Gibbs, 1999

> Schools cannot expect their students to learn the lessons of good citizenship when school authorities themselves disregard the fundamental principles underpinning our constitutional freedoms.
> —Justice William Brennan,
> dissenting in *Doe v. Renfrow*, 1981

Randall R. Beger, "Expansion of Police Power in Public Schools and the Vanishing Rights of Students," *Social Justice*, Spring/Summer 2002, p. 119. Copyright © 2000 by Crime and Social Justice Associates. Reproduced by permission.

G rowing public anxiety over acts of violence in schools has prompted educators and state lawmakers to adopt drastic measures to improve the safety of students. In the wake of recent high-profile campus shootings, schools have become almost prison-like in terms of security and in diminishing the rights of students. Ironically, a repressive approach to school safety may do more harm than good by creating an atmosphere of mistrust and alienation that causes students to misbehave.

Schools have become almost prison-like.

This article examines law enforcement expansion in schools and the vanishing Fourth Amendment rights of public school children. The climate of fear generated by recent school shootings has spurred school administrators to increase security through physical means (locks, surveillance cameras, metal detectors) and to hire more police and security guards. State lawmakers have eagerly jumped on the school safety bandwagon by making it easier to punish school children as adults for a wide range of offenses that traditionally have been handled informally by teachers. Instead of safeguarding the rights of students against arbitrary police power, our nation's courts are granting police and school officials more authority to conduct searches of students. Tragically, little if any Fourth Amendment protection now exists to shield students from the raw exercise of police power in public schools.

The new school security culture

In response to the latest string of sensationalized school shootings, schools everywhere have made safety a top priority. A recent U.S. Department of Education survey of public schools found that 96% required guests to sign in before entering the school building, 80% had a closed campus policy that forbids students to leave campus for lunch, and 53% controlled access to their school buildings. A National School Board Association survey of over 700 school districts throughout the United States found that 39% of urban school districts use metal detectors, 75% use locker searches, and 65% use security personnel. Schools have introduced stricter dress codes, put up barbed-wire security fences, banned book bags and pagers, and have added "lock down drills" and "SWAT team" rehearsals to their safety programs. Officials in Dallas, Texas, unveiled a $41 million state-of-the art "security conscious" school that has 37 surveillance cameras, six metal detectors, and a security command center for monitoring the building and grounds. At Tewksbury Memorial High School in Massachusetts, 20 video cameras bring the school into the local police department via remote access technology. According to [*Current Events*], "the video cameras record almost everything students say and do at school—eating in the cafeteria, cramming in the library, chatting in the halls." The new security culture in public schools has stirred debate over whether schools have turned into "learning prisons" where the students unwittingly become "guinea pigs" to test the latest security devices, [according to Gail R. Chaddock].

Since the mid-1990s, a growing number of schools have adopted zero tolerance policies under which students receive predetermined penalties for any offense, no matter how minor. Students have been expelled or suspended from school for sharing aspirin, Midol, and Certs tablets, and for bringing nail clippers and scissors to class. There is no credible evidence that zero tolerance measures improve classroom management or the behavior of students. Such measures are not only ineffectual, but also appear to have a negative impact on children of color. Research indicates that black children are more likely than are whites to be expelled or suspended from school under zero tolerance.

Schools are safe

Although most Americans believe that public schools are violent and dangerous places, numerous surveys on school safety contradict this notion. For example, according to U.S. Department of Education statistics, only 10% of public schools experienced one or more serious violent crimes during the 1996–1997 school year. Over the same period, almost half the nation's public schools (43%) reported no incidents of serious crime. Data from the Uniform Crime Reports show a decline of approximately 56% in juvenile homicide arrests between 1993 and 1998. In *Justice Blind? Ideals and Realities of American Criminal Justice*, Matthew Robinson explains why the conventional wisdom that schools are dangerous places is irrational:

> There are more than 51 million students and approximately 3 million teachers in American schools. In 1996, there were approximately 380,000 violent victimizations at school against these roughly 54 million people. This means the rate of violent victimization at U.S. schools is about 704 per 100,000 people. Stated differently, about 0.7% of people can expect to become victims of serious violent crimes at schools.

The odds of a child being killed at school by gunfire during the 1998–1999 school year were about one in two million. Contrary to media hyperbole about violence in public schools, most school-related injuries are nonviolent in nature, and the majority of crimes that occur in schools are thefts.

The police buildup in public schools

Despite the relative rarity of school violence, officials everywhere are feeling pressure to improve the safety of students and staff. An increasingly popular "quick fix" strategy is to hire police and security guards. According to a U.S. Department of Education study, about 19% of public schools had the full-time presence of a police officer or other law enforcement representative during the 1996–1997 school year.

School police officers take many forms. Some are regular uniformed police officers working on a part-time basis for a school district. Others are hired and trained by school security departments. In New York City alone, some 3,200 uniformed school security officers work in the Division of School Safety of the City Board of Education, "a contingent larger than the Boston Police Department," [according to John Devine]. Many school districts use more than one form of police, such as campus police with support from local police or private security guards.

The odds of a child being killed at school by gunfire during the 1998–1999 school year were about one in two million.

School Resource Officers (SROs) are the fastest-growing segment of law enforcement officials stationed in public schools. These armed and uniformed law enforcement officials perform multiple tasks, such as patrolling school grounds, assisting with investigations of students who break school rules, and arresting students who commit crimes. SROs also perform nontraditional law enforcement functions that include chaperoning dances, counseling students, and conducting seminars on substance abuse prevention. In 1997, there were 9,446 School Resource Officers in local police departments assigned to public schools in the United States. Their numbers have increased rapidly in recent years due to increased funding at the federal level to hire more officers. [Between 2000 and 2002], the Office of Community Oriented Policing Services (COPS) awarded more than $350 million in grants to the COPS in Schools program to hire over 3,200 School Resource Officers at an annual cost of $54,687 each. Under a federal budget plan supported by President George W. Bush, COPS funding to hire school police will more than double.

The large influx of police officers in public schools has shifted the responsibility for maintaining order and discipline in the classroom away from teachers and into the hands of law enforcement officials. In *Maximum Security: The Culture of Violence in Inner-City Schools*, John Devine describes how school security police in New York public schools have "taken on an independent existence, with [their] own organization and procedures, language, rules, equipment, dressing rooms, uniforms, vans, and lines of authority." A school principal admitted to Devine: "I have no control over security guards, they don't report to me." Recently, the New York City Board of Education, at the urging of former Mayor Rudolf Giuliani, voted to transfer responsibility for school safety to the city police. School boards in other states, including California, Florida, and Nevada, have come out in favor of placing student safety under the control of city police.

Lawmakers support police presence in schools

The trend in support of moving school discipline in the direction of law enforcement has also been given a push by state lawmakers. In Arizona, for example, a new state law requires that school officials report any crimes or security threats involving students to the local police. Under a new Michigan statute, teachers must involve the police in any search of students' lockers, cars, and personal belongings. The law explicitly states that evidence obtained from a search by a police officer cannot be excluded in a court or school disciplinary hearing. States have also enacted legislation that requires school officials to share information about students with police, including personal information gathered by school therapists and counselors.

Concurrently, state lawmakers have dramatically increased the penalties for crimes committed on school property. In Mississippi, the penalty for having a gun on school property is a fine of up to $5,000 and up to three years in prison. Louisiana law prescribes that any student or non-student carrying a firearm on school grounds "shall be imprisoned at hard labor for not more than five years." Most states have also increased the penalties for selling or using drugs on school campuses. Laws in Illinois, New Hampshire, and Michigan call for severe penalties, including imprisonment, for the possession or distribution of drugs in or near schools and have lowered the current age for prosecution of juveniles as adults. Under recent "zero tolerance" initiatives, trivial forms of student misconduct that were once handled informally by teachers and school administrators are now more likely to result in police arrest and referral to juvenile or adult court. Five students in Mississippi were suspended recently and criminally charged for tossing peanuts at each other on a school bus, a peanut hit the bus driver by mistake.

Searches and stings

Increasingly, the search efforts of police officials stationed in public schools mirror the actions of prison guards. For example, to create a drug-free environment, schools are allowing police officers to conduct random preemptive searches of students' lockers and personal property using specially trained sniff dogs. Over 1,000 schools in 14 states use drug-sniffing dogs supplied by a Texas company called Interquest Detection Canines. The profit motive is a powerful incentive to expand canine searches to schools that have no demonstrable drug problems. One school board has even formed a partnership with the U.S. Customs Department to send dogs into classrooms for drug-detection training exercises. In writing about canine searches in Boston public schools, journalist Marcia Vigue describes the following scene:

> Secrecy is the key. Students, teachers, and parents are not warned in advance; some student handbooks do not even explain that [searches] might occur from time to time. . . . During the searches, the dogs respond to German commands like "sook"—which means search—by pushing their snouts against lockers and nudging their noses into bags and coats. Sometimes, after students have been told to leave, the dogs pass through classrooms and other rooms to sniff students' belongings.

The personal indignity of forcing students to submit to a suspicion-less canine search is something no adult would tolerate.

Besides police controlled canine searches, schools are turning to sting operations in which undercover law enforcement officials pretend to be students to conduct actual criminal investigations of students suspected of using or dealing drugs in the school setting. In Los Angeles, for example, undercover officers made over 200 drug buys over a five-month period at local schools. Opponents of school-based sting operations say they not only create a climate of mistrust between students and police, but also put innocent students at risk of wrongful arrest due to faulty tips and overzealous police work. When asked about his role in a recent undercover drug probe at a high school near Atlanta, a young-looking police officer who attended classes and went to parties with students replied: "I knew I had to fit in, make the kids trust me and then turn around and take them to jail."

Schools are allowing police officers to conduct random preemptive searches of students' lockers and personal property.

Police have adopted other aggressive search tactics on school campuses, such as herding students into hallways for unannounced weapons searches, known as "blitz operations." At Shawnee Heights and Seaman High School in Kansas City, signs warn students driving into school parking areas that they have just consented to searches of their vehicles "with or without cause" by school administrators or police officers. Scores of other schools across the country have adopted similar vehicle search policies. Groups of students have even been strip-searched by police officers to locate money missing from a classroom. There seems to be no end in sight to the aggressive search methods police are willing to use on students in the name of safety.

The Fourth Amendment and schools

The Fourth Amendment of the United States Constitution provides the following:

> The right of the people to be secure in their persons, houses, papers, and effects against unreasonable searches and seizures, shall not be violated, and no Warrants shall issue, but upon probable cause, supported by Oath or affirmation, and particularly describing the place to be searched, and the persons or things to be seized.

In the past, courts held that school authorities acted in loco parentis [in the place of a parent] when searching students and as such were not bound by Fourth Amendment restrictions that apply to state officials.

In the 1995 landmark case of *New Jersey v. T.L.O.*, the United States Supreme Court held that the Fourth Amendment did apply to searches conducted by public school officials. The Court specifically considered the search of a student's purse by an assistant vice-principal after a teacher had discovered the student, and her friend, smoking in the school washroom in violation of school policy. Upon searching T.L.O.'s purse, the assistant vice-principal discovered cigarettes and a package of cigarette rolling papers, which to him suggested involvement with marijuana. A more extensive search revealed a small amount of marijuana, a pipe, empty plastic bags, and letters implicating T.L.O. in selling drugs. Thereafter, the police were notified and the state of New Jersey filed delinquency charges against

T.L.O. for possession of marijuana with intent to sell.

On appeal, the U.S Supreme Court ruled that school children do not waive their Fourth Amendment rights by bringing purses, books, and items necessary for personal grooming and hygiene to school. However, a certain degree of "flexibility" in school searches was deemed necessary, which made the warrant and probable cause requirements "impractical." Ultimately, the Court held that school officials need only have "reasonable suspicion" for student searches. Reasonable suspicion means that school officials "must have some [articulable] facts or knowledge that provide reasonable grounds" before conducting a search [according to Richard Lawrence, author of *School Crime and Juvenile Justice*]. Under *T.L.O.*, a search is reasonable if, first, the search decision is supported by reasonable suspicion and, second, the scope of the search is not "excessively intrusive" in light of the age and sex of the student and the nature of the infraction.

People v. Dilworth

The *T.L.O.* decision avoided the issue of whether the probable cause or reasonable suspicion standard would apply to police searches in public schools. In the absence of a clear standard to guide police searches on school campuses, appellate courts have fashioned new criteria that give police officers the same search leeway as teachers. The case examined below, *People v. Dilworth*, is a good example.

Courts have given law enforcement officials the widest latitude to search students.

Kenneth Dilworth, a 15-year-old high school student in Joliet, Illinois, was arrested for drug possession by a police detective assigned full-time to a high school for teenagers with behavioral disorders. Detective Francis Ruettiger served as liaison police officer on staff at the school, but was employed by the Joliet police department. Two teachers at the school asked Ruettiger to search a student, Deshawn Weeks, for drugs. The teachers informed Ruettiger that they had overheard Weeks telling other students he had sold some drugs and would bring more drugs with him to school the next day. The detective searched Weeks, but no drugs were found. Ruettiger then escorted the boy to his locker, where the youth and 15-year-old Kenneth Dilworth began talking and giggling. Ruettiger testified he felt "like [he] was being played for a fool." The officer noticed Dilworth had a flashlight and suspected it might contain contraband. He seized it, unscrewed the top, and found cocaine. After discovering cocaine, Ruettiger chased and captured Dilworth, handcuffed him, placed him in a police vehicle, and escorted him to the Joliet police station. Dilworth was subsequently tried and found guilty in adult court for unlawful possession of a controlled substance with intent to deliver on school property. He was sentenced to a four-year term of imprisonment. Dilworth's motion to reconsider the sentence was denied.

The appellate court reversed Dilworth's conviction on the grounds that his motion to suppress evidence discovered in his flashlight should have been granted. In the opinion of the appellate court, Ruettiger's seizure and search of the flashlight were based on only an unparticularized suspicion or "hunch" and did not comport with any standard of reasonableness for searches and seizures of students and their effects by state officials.

However, a divided Illinois Supreme Court in a four-to-three decision reversed the appellate court decision. Claiming that a flashlight in the context of an alternative school could reasonably be construed to be a weapon, the court affirmed Ruettiger's search as reasonable. The majority reasoned that lower expectations of privacy in the school setting, discussed in *T.L.O.*, supported a sharp departure from the probable cause standard for a school liaison officer. Even though detective Ruettiger was employed by the Joliet police department and performed duties at the school more in line with a regular law enforcement officer than a school official, the court maintained the search was proper.

Violating probable cause

The Dilworth decision stands in stark opposition to Fourth Amendment precedents that require the probable cause test to be met when evidence from a search by a law enforcement official forms the basis of a criminal prosecution. For example, in *A.J.M v. State* (1993), the *T.L.O.* standard does not apply to a search by a sheriff's officer who was serving as a school resource officer and was asked to conduct a search by the school principal; in *F.P. v. State* (1988), the *T.L.O.* standard does not apply where a search is carried out at the behest of police.

Justice Nickels, dissenting in *Dilworth*, severely criticized the majority for lowering the search standard for a school police officer when he stated:

> I cannot agree with the majority that a police officer whose self-stated primary duty is to investigate and prevent criminal activity may search a student on school grounds on a lesser [F]ourth amendment standard than probable cause merely because the police officer is permanently assigned to the school and is listed in the student handbook as a member of the school staff. The majority's departure from a unanimous line of Federal and State decisions places form over substance and opens the door for widespread abuse and erosion of students' [F]ourth amendment rights to be free from unreasonable searches and seizures by law enforcement officers.

The Dilworth decision is representative of a series of recent cases in which trial and appellate courts have lowered the bar for student searches by police officers. Instead of protecting schoolchildren from arbitrary police intrusion, courts have given law enforcement officials the widest latitude to search students. For example, state appellate courts have redefined police search conduct as "minor" or "incidental" to justify application of the reasonable suspicion standard. Appellate courts have also suggested that the lesser reasonable suspicion test should be applied when police search at the request of school officials or are present when school authorities engage in a search. Courts have even upheld dragnet suspicionless searches of school lockers and police-directed canine searches of students' property with no warnings. Due to these decisions, public school children may now be searched on less than probable cause and prosecuted in adult court with the evidence from the search

Diminishing the rights of students

In response to widely publicized incidents of schoolyard violence, public schools have adopted rigid and intrusive security measures that diminish the rights of students. In the name of safety, students are being spied on with hidden cameras, searched without suspicion, and subjected to unannounced locker searches by police with drug-sniffing dogs. Concurrently, federal and state lawmakers have significantly increased penalties for crimes committed on school property. Trivial forms of student misconduct that used to be handled informally by teachers and school administrators are now more likely to result in arrest and referral to a juvenile or adult court. Ironically, the current "crackdown" on schoolchildren comes at a time when the level of violence and drug use in public schools has gone down.

Because the school setting demands "constant submission to authority" [in the words of Mai Linh Spencer] and is imposing harsher criminal penalties on students who misbehave, the legal rights of schoolchildren ought to be given the highest legal protection afforded by the nation's courts. Regrettably, the opposite is true. Bowing to public fears and legislative pressures, trial and appellate courts have reduced the Fourth Amendment rights of students to an abstraction. The nation's courts no longer seem interested in scrutinizing the specific facts surrounding the search of a student to determine if police had probable cause or even reasonable suspicion. Instead, courts search for a policy justification—e.g, minimizing disruptions to school order or protecting the safety of students and teachers—to uphold the search, even when police use evidence seized under lower and increasingly porous search standards to convict minors in adult criminal court. Given the current atmosphere of widespread fear and distress precipitated by the September 11, 2001, tragedy there is little reason to expect courts will impose any restrictions on searches in schools. Ironically, children are unsafe in public schools today not because of exposure to drugs and violence, but because they have lost their constitutional protections under the Fourth Amendment.

7

Increased Gun Control Can Prevent School Shootings

Lionel Van Deerlin

Lionel Van Deerlin, a former congressman, is a columnist for the San Diego Union-Tribune.

Recent shootings at the nation's schools reveal that guns are too easy for young people to acquire. Despite such evidence to the contrary, gun enthusiasts insist that current gun control laws are adequate. In fact, existing gun control laws contain loopholes that allow guns to circulate untraced and permit people to own large numbers of weapons. In addition, purchasers are able to obtain firearms at gun shows without background checks. Gun laws must be strengthened to prevent more school shootings.

The school tragedy in Santee [California, where fifteen-year-old Andy Williams killed two and injured thirteen] revives a nagging question. What's to be done about lethal weapons in the hands of persons who should not have them?

Little or nothing, it would seem.

Perhaps the unlikelihood we'd ever get more workable firearms laws was forecast by an earlier gun-related incident in this same suburb a dozen years ago.

That's when a sailor stepped into a crowded Santee bar brandishing what turned out to be a toy gun. In the tense situation that ensued, several other bar patrons produced real guns.

No shooting occurred, but everyone agreed a highly dangerous situation had been averted. And so Santee's city council acted—to bar toy guns.

Why no gun control?

In more recent times, from Littleton, Colo. [where students Eric Harris and Dylan Klebold went on a shooting rampage, killing fifteen, including themselves], to Santee, we have witnessed a repeated slaughter of the innocents with weapons—real ones—all too easily accessed by troubled

Lionel Van Deerlin, "Becoming Prisoners of Our Own Gun Culture," *San Diego Union-Tribune*, March 14, 2001, p. B7. Copyright © 2001 by the San Diego Union-Tribune Publishing Company. Reproduced by permission of the author.

kids. And yet the chances seem diminishing that anything will be done about it. Why?

For one thing, of course, we now have a national administration, along with a Congress, committed to the mantra you'd find on any of those provocative bumper stickers from the National Rifle Association. Even allowing for the exuberance of an NRA operative who bragged that the organization soon would have a desk in the Oval Office, it's clear that the new president [George W. Bush] and his attorney general [John Ashcroft] do not intend tightening gun laws.

If we must register our automobiles, why not our guns?

Asked what else we might do to curtail these school shootings, President Bush said it's up to parents to teach their kids right from wrong.

This, it seems to me, is as uncertain as his proposed missile defense plan to deflect incoming missiles. Suppose we stop the first 40 or 50—the 51st can still shoot up the schoolyard.

Today's spirit of frustration, alas, trickles down from Washington. San Diego Sheriff Bill Kolender, an outspoken advocate of tougher gun control when a candidate for office, is now quoted as saying, "You can't think guns are going away. They're not."

For those NRA types, the classic definition of gun control remains: a steady aim. New laws? Don't be absurd, they'll say. Look at the multitude of regulations already available to law enforcement. If these have not stopped the violence, how will new laws help?

Regrettably, there are more than enough loopholes to match every law on the books. Consider our early inability to trace ownership of the German-made revolver used in wreaking havoc at Santana High.

Donald R. Kincaid, special agent in charge of regional operations for the Bureau of Alcohol, Tobacco & Firearms, knows the weapon was shipped to the United States nearly 10 years before accused shooter Charles Andrew Williams was born. But agents could not determine a chain of ownership after its initial purchase—which occurred long before this gun became the property of Andy's father.

Registration and licensing would take care of that. If we must register our automobiles, why not our guns? Would this not discourage a traffic that too often turns deadly?

And since we're in question time—could Williams senior show a real need for all eight of those firearms that were said to be on his premises?

Gun shows and the Second Amendment

The Brady law (which the NRA still hopes to emasculate) has denied gun sales to hundreds of criminals, minors and mentally incompetents. Still, one needn't be an unreasonable worrywart to ask why restrictions over gun shows continue to leave an enforcement gap wide enough for a Sherman tank. The deaths at Columbine High, remember, were inflicted with weapons acquired, unchecked, at gun shows.

(Though it hosts none of these gun shows, Santee's 2 percent of the county's population supports no fewer than three gun shops, fully 12 percent of those listed in the Yellow Pages.)

Finally, we must contend anew with the Second Amendment, the constitutional underpinning for everyone's right to bear arms. And we see how bleak this entitlement has become. The "well regulated militia" rightly shielded in colonial days emerges now as a frightened 15-year-old aiming to square accounts with schoolground tormentors.

Some in Santee are asking why. Van Collinsworth relays a deadly toll he extracted from the Internet. In the most recent compilation for a single year, Collinsworth finds, no children reportedly died from firearms in Japan, against 19 in Great Britain, 57 in Germany, 109 in France, 153 in Canada—and 5,285 in the United States.

So, these final questions: Are we Americans truly the most violent, the deadliest people among all industrial nations?

Or just the stupidest?

8

Gun Control Will Not Prevent School Shootings

Joseph Perkins

Joseph Perkins is an editorial writer for the San Diego Union-Tribune.

Increased gun control will not end school shootings because guns are not the cause of the problem. Young people have always had access to guns but have only recently started bringing them to school and shooting their classmates. The true cause of the shootings is the violent content of video games, movies, television shows, and music lyrics to which young people are exposed. More gun control will do nothing to change this culture of violence that teaches children a casual attitude toward mayhem and killing.

Andy Williams spent his Wednesday [March 7, 2001] afternoon in a San Diego County courtroom. The 15-year-old was charged with gunning down two of his classmates at Santana High School and wounding 13 others.

"Why?" asked the teachers who taught him, the police who arrested him, the prosecutors who charged him, and the media horde that covered him.

Jeff Cody spent his Wednesday evening at Dave & Busters, a national "food and entertainment" chain that just opened a San Diego location. It's quite popular with virtual-reality and video game junkies.

So 11-year-old Jeff spent a matter of hours with ersatz weaponry in his hands, gunning down human targets on really cool video games. Like Sega's "L.A. Machine Gun," in which the president of the United States is subject to an armed assault. And Konami's "Silent Scope," in which the player is transmogrified into a sniper.

Between games, the fifth grader pondered whether exposure to violent video games might contribute to school shootings, like the one up the road at Santana High. "Maybe, a little," he responded.

Meanwhile, the "search for answers" in the Santana High shootings continues. Is the boy the product of a dysfunctional family? Does he have

Joseph Perkins, "Don't Blame Guns for the Santana High Tragedy," *San Diego Union-Tribune*, March 9, 2001, p. B7. Copyright © 2001 by the San Diego Union-Tribune Publishing Company. Reproduced by permission of the author.

a history of mental illness? Is there a substance abuse problem? Was he tired of being bullied?

So far, none of these possibilities has panned out.

It's hard to imagine any new gun control law that would have prevented the carnage at Santana High.

His single, divorced dad had not physically abused him or sexually molested him or anything like that. The ninth grader wasn't seeing a shrink, hadn't been previously diagnosed with any mental problems. He wasn't drug or alcohol addled at the time of the shooting. And he had no beef with the kids he randomly shot.

The usual culprit

So the school-shootings "experts" have settled on the usual culprit—the gun.

If only there were not so many guns in this country. If only guns were not so easily acquired by kids. If only gun-owning parents kept their weapons locked up. If only there were more gun-control laws.

Well, yes, there are a lot of guns in this country, somewhere between 200 million and 250 million. But Americans have been armed to the teeth since the nation's very founding. Yet the rash of underage gun violence, particularly on school campuses, is a fairly recent phenomenon.

Yes, there have been national surveys suggesting that more than half of middle school and high school students know how and where to purchase a firearm.

But most licensed gun dealers are law-abiding business folk, contrary to prevailing myth. If a minor tried to buy a gun from them, tried to get them to commit an obvious felony, they would toss him out on his underaged ear.

No, the accused reportedly "borrowed" his dad's gun, locked away in a cabinet. Apparently, he was determined to get the weapon, locked up or not. And a trigger lock probably would have been no more of a deterrent.

America's culture of violence

It's hard to imagine any new gun control law that would have prevented the carnage at Santana High. For the problem is not the gun, it is America's culture of violence.

Indeed, America's youth are inured to violence through saturation exposure to violence-laden video games—like those at Dave & Busters—and movies and television and music.

Before the average American child finishes elementary school, he or she will view 100,000 acts of violence on television including 8,000 murders.

Then when they get old enough to go to the movies by themselves, they are exposed to even more violence. In fact, the Federal Trade Commission issued a report [in 2000] finding that movie studios "routinely undercut their own rating restrictions by targeting marketing violent films . . . to young audiences."

The music industry is no different. When kids go to Wherehouse or Tower Records, they see in-store promotions—sponsored by record companies—for the latest CDs featuring hard core, violence-glorifying lyrics. Record execs insist they behave responsibly because they affix parental warning labels on their violent product.

But parents don't really know what their kids are listening to. And record companies know it. Because parents may hear a cleaned-up version of a certain artist's music on the radio and feel comfortable allowing their youngsters to purchase the artist's CD. But the music store sells the kid the uncensored CD—unbeknownst to their parents—violent lyrics intact.

Against this backdrop, it is easy to understand how, according to police, the accused shooter could show no obvious signs of being distraught, disturbed or under great emotional stress after blowing away his classmates.

Violence came as naturally to the teen-age shooter as grooving to his Walkman, catching a movie, checking out the tube, or playing a video game.

9

Using Students as Metal Detectors

Ana Figueroa and Adam Rogers

Ana Figueroa is a staff reporter for Newsweek *magazine. Adam Rogers is a general editor for* Newsweek.

Most school shooters talk about their desire to commit violence prior to acting on it. Often their comments are not taken seriously. In order to prevent school shootings, students should be encouraged to report to authorities all threats of violence, however innocent they may seem. Financial incentives can help to break down the cultural resistance to "tattling" and create an atmosphere in which it is considered acceptable to speak up about a potentially violent peer.

Neil O'Grady laughed when he heard about it. "Andy talked for a while about getting a gun and bringing it to school to shoot people," said the Santana High School 15-year-old of his close friend, Charles Andrew Williams. "He even told me to stay home Monday, but I just sort of laughed, because I thought it was a joke. He likes to joke around a lot." Josh Stevens, another good friend, also dismissed the threats, which he believes Williams shared with "20 or 30 people." That in itself was reason not to worry, Stevens reasoned: "If he was serious, you wouldn't think he'd tell people."

Andy Williams, it seems, was the kind of kid no one took too seriously. Skinny and jug-eared, he was teased by the older teens at Woodglen Vista Park, where he would hang out to ride his skateboard and smoke pot. "We'd tell him to shut up and sit down, and he'd just do it," says Jessie Cunard, 18, a dropout from Santana himself. "People stole his shoes and skateboard and other stuff, and he just let them." Raised in small towns in the East, Williams was ill at ease in Santee, Calif., a suburb on the far fringes of San Diego, where he moved with his divorced father last summer. To his friends back in Brunswick, Md., where he lived until 1999, he would complain about the casual brutality of a teenage culture in which any display of vulnerability marked you as a "faggot." "He got

Ana Figueroa and Adam Rogers, "Using Students as Metal Detectors: Tattling May Be the Only Way to Stop the Next Santee," *Newsweek*, March 19, 2001, p. 28. Copyright © 2001 by Newsweek, Inc. All rights reserved. Reproduced by permission.

a haircut and they beat him up," says Mary Neiderlander, whose daughter, Kathleen Seek, had a brief moment of celebrity as Williams's former girlfriend. But although school officials were still checking their records last week, Williams apparently didn't impress most adults as the kind of alienated loner who bore watching. "Even the week before the shooting, Andy was a great, loving and fun guy," says Ashley Petersen, a 14-year-old from the neighborhood. Which is why even the people he'd told about it were shocked on Monday when, according to police, Williams pulled out an eight-shot, .22-caliber handgun and began firing in a boys' bathroom, killing two students and wounding 13, including two adults.

"Snitching is becoming cool."

What is amazing is that, almost two years after the appalling bloodbath of Columbine, no one thought to warn authorities. And it's not because the school was indifferent to the danger. Congress has all but given up on tougher gun-control laws, so Santana, like many schools, has taken matters into its own hands. Or, rather, put it in the hands of students, who are being asked to bear the brunt of responsibility for their own safety, on the theory that "students are the best metal detectors," in the words of school-board president Daniel McGeorge. The school offers peer counseling, conflict-resolution classes and seminars in tolerance. Each September, vice principals meet individually with each of the 1,900 students to urge them to come forward—anonymously, if they wish—with information about potential threats from classmates. In retrospect, of course, those in whom Williams confided now wish they'd been a little less sure he was joking. "I kind of feel like I'm to blame for some of this because I could have done something," says Chris Reynolds, the adult boyfriend of Josh Stevens's mother, who heard about the plan two days before the shooting. Reynolds said the youth told him he wasn't serious. Four students who heard Williams talk about shooting up the school, including Stevens and O'Grady, have been suspended for the rest of the school year—for their own safety, school officials say, after threats were made against them.

Obviously, teenage culture has a strong bias against informing. "No one wants the stigma of being a squealer," says Charles Ewing, the author of "When Children Kill." (Ewing estimates that 60 to 70 percent of school shooters talked about their killings in advance, and so in theory could have been stopped.) Teens in southern California use "to narc" as a generic synonym for "to inform," which suggests that they have lost sight of the difference between turning in a friend for smoking pot and alerting authorities that someone is carrying a shotgun. But even adult society has trouble with this concept sometimes. Last week a California legislator proposed a bill to give legal protection to students who report threats. It was prompted by a case in which the parents of a student who was suspended for allegedly making threats sued the child who turned him in. The suit was eventually dismissed, according to news reports, but it cost the second family $40,000 in legal bills.

To break through the stigma, school authorities are rethinking incentives. One way to encourage informing is to pay for it, which is the premise of Crime Stoppers—a program of rewards for tipping off the police that has now spread to an estimated 3,000 schools around the country. In the three years it's been underway in Tampa, Fla., 48 weapons have been recovered, including eight firearms. Detective Lisa Haber, who runs the program, says the rewards are often not even picked up. What matters is creating a climate in which it's OK to go to the authorities, especially with the promise of anonymity. "Snitching is becoming cool," says James Alan Fox, a nationally recognized criminologist. "Ten years ago if you said 'I'm bringing a gun to school,' the reaction would have been 'Yeah, right.' Now it is taken seriously." Within days of Williams's rampage, authorities made eight arrests after receiving tips from students about potential threats at five different schools in southern California. But Santana, still coping with the grief and havoc wreaked by one child's unfathomable rage, could only wish someone had taken Andy Williams seriously.

10

Identifying At-Risk Students Can Help Prevent School Violence

James M. Kauffman

James M. Kauffman is a professor emeritus of education at the University of Virginia and the author of several books on special education.

School officials often do not recognize that a student is having emotional problems until it is too late and a catastrophe—such as a school shooting—has occurred. To remedy this problem, educators should use screening techniques to identify students who are at risk of engaging in violence or other inappropriate behavior. These students can then be given clear instructions regarding appropriate behavior. Officials should also provide all students with reasonable punishment for unacceptable behavior and praise and recognition for good behavior. Only by intervening before tragedy strikes can schools be made safe for all students.

Unlike psychological testing, behavioral screening does not delve into the student's mental life or psychological processes. It is merely a process of identifying students who are most likely to cause trouble to others and themselves. Public schools should use behavioral screening, but only if they follow it with actions shown to reduce the likelihood of problem behavior. By "problem behavior" I mean behavior that is very likely to be judged unacceptable or maladaptive—fighting, intimidating others, mean-spirited teasing, disobedience to adults, disrespectful conduct, extreme social withdrawal and other ways of demonstrating a lack of social awareness or congeniality.

Some public schools have become places where obstreperous, mean, disrespectful, intimidating behavior is treated as "okay" and "normal." Properly implemented behavioral screening identifies students whose behavior is unacceptable, even if they are just starting to exhibit such bad conduct. And, if it is followed by best behavior-management practices,

James M. Kauffman, "Q: Should Schools Use Behavioral Screening to Find 'At-Risk' Children? Yes: Kids with Serious Emotional Problems Need to Be Identified Early On and Helped," *Insight*, October 4–11, 1999, pp. 40–43. Copyright © 2004 by News World Communications, Inc. All rights reserved. Reprinted by permission.

behavioral screening allows teachers to nip these problems in the bud—to prevent them from escalating into something worse. ☆

Most teachers know which students probably are headed for trouble. However, most problem students aren't formally identified until they are about 15 years old and their problems are longstanding and severe—way too late for prevention. Teachers do better in identifying high-risk youngsters of any age when they have a systematic way of describing kids' behavior and know just what to look for. The most accurate and reliable behavioral screening methods rely on teacher judgments guided by rating and observation instruments that have been field-tested. The best such instruments are the SSBD (Systematic Screening for Behavior Disorders) and the ESP (Early Screening Project), created and field-tested by educational researcher Hill M. Walker and his associates at the University of Oregon. Some school districts have purchased these instruments or adopted behavioral-screening policies. However, I do not know—and I doubt anyone does—which districts or states have attempted to implement behavioral screening and related preventive practices as field-tested and recommended by Walker and his colleagues or other prominent scientists.

The essential question

Here's the essential question you have to ask when you weigh the pros and cons of behavioral screening: Would I rather let problems become intolerable before doing something about them or, alternatively, identify problems when they're not so bad and prevent them from getting worse? The simple fact is that you can't prevent something after it happens. Either you prevent it or you let it happen and then bemoan it.

The only reason to use behavioral screening in schools is prevention. School personnel and the general public increasingly call for the prevention of school shootings and other outrageous acts of violence. Preventing such incidents would save a lot of money, not to mention lives and misery. But ignorance and politics stand in the way. So we wait for catastrophe, then ask why it happened. Here are some arguments people trot out to defeat prevention, even while saying they want it. I discuss these in detail in "How We Prevent the Prevention of Emotional and Behavioral Disorders" in the journal *Exceptional Children* (Summer 1999).

Public schools should use behavioral screening, but only if they follow it with actions shown to reduce the likelihood of problem behavior.

We don't want to label and stigmatize kids. You can't prevent what you can't talk about, and you can't talk about something without a label for it. Furthermore, there is no credible evidence that labels and stigma are the problem. Kids behave badly, then get labeled—not the other way around. And those who feel no guilt, those who experience no stigma attached to unacceptable behavior, are more likely headed for bigger trouble than those who do.

We don't want to "medicalize" or "psychologize" the problem. We haven't.

We have made it a legal problem. False accusation, privacy, due process and other legal matters are the objections people tend to raise.

Gambling on the side of caution

False positives are unacceptable. Every screening device produces some errors: false positives and false negatives. A false positive means the screening identifies someone it shouldn't have; a false negative means someone who should have been identified was overlooked. Which kind of error is more dangerous? It depends on the consequences. False positives—for example, false convictions—are what judges and juries try hardest to avoid. False negatives, which involve overlooking illnesses, are the dangers doctors worry about most. Legally, we worry most about personal rights; medically, we worry most about health and safety. Educators, like physicians, should choose to be safe rather than sorry. In *Consilience: The Unity of Knowledge*, Edward O. Wilson puts it this way: "In ecology, as in medicine, a false positive diagnosis is an inconvenience, but a false negative diagnosis can be catastrophic. That is why ecologists and doctors don't like to gamble at all, and if they must, it is always on the side of caution. It is a mistake to dismiss a worried ecologist or a worried doctor as an alarmist." It is also a mistake to dismiss a worried teacher as an alarmist. Too often, educators' worries are dismissed until the problem is severe. Then, of course, it is too late for prevention, and the action demanded by the public and the law is suspension, expulsion or imprisonment.

Special education and related interventions don't work. Screening may result in special education or related services, such as counseling. Special education can and often does work well in preventing the catastrophic consequences of academic failure and unchecked misbehavior. Of course anything can be poorly implemented, producing bad results. But when special education and related programs are conducted well, identifying the students who need them and providing the services do more good than harm. False positives aren't as dangerous as false negatives.

We don't want to place any student in a restrictive environment. Every place is restrictive of some things and not of others. Schools should restrict bad behavior in an effective and humane way. Students should be placed in classes and schools where their unacceptable behavior and academic failure are restricted and their desirable conduct and academic learning effectively are encouraged.

We don't want to identify more students for special services; we already serve too many. If you want to prevent problems, then you have to identify more kids—address problems earlier, which inevitably means identifying more students than we do now, when we wait for the problems to get out of hand.

Special education and related services cost too much. You have to spend more now on screening and prevention to save money in the long run. Prevention isn't free any way you cut it, but it's cheaper than the alternative. Most Americans, including elected representatives, don't take the long view. They'd rather have low taxes now or even tax cuts and ostensible legal protections than spend money on prevention that would save dollars down the road and make schools safer. Whose fault? We elect our representatives.

Don't worry; this kid will grow out of it. Such "developmental optimism" isn't often warranted in the case of aggressive, disruptive, disobedient, intimidating, can't-pay-attention behavior. All the evidence indicates this kind of behavior is poison for a child's future—likely to get worse without appropriate management.

Too many minority kids get identified. Too few kids of every ethnic group are identified. The evidence is overwhelming that any observed disproportion in identification is not a result of overidentification of minority students but underidentification of others. *Diversity is to be welcomed, and deviance is in the eye of the beholder.* Difference is not necessarily deviance. But some kinds of diversity are not okay, especially the disruption, aggression, academic failure, inattention, disobedience and disrespect that are the primary targets of behavioral screening. Deviance is behavior that leads to unacceptable later outcomes, and we can define it away or deal with it as a reality.

But, let's suppose that a school, district or state decides to do behavioral screening, using a field-tested instrument such as the SSBD or ESP to guide the selection of kids at risk for worsening problems. Let's suppose they stay faithfully with the user's manual so that false positives and false negatives are minimized and the vast majority of the students identified by the screening really are headed for bigger trouble if we don't do something now. What should we do?

The popular view is that punishment is the key. Hammer them early with humiliation if not corporal punishment. Wrong. This is not smart for the long term. The real key is a highly structured program, instruction that lets kids know what's okay and what is not, that provides consistent positive and negative consequences for behavior. But, like anything else, if it's done poorly, it'll turn out badly.

If you want behavioral screening and prevention to work, then you have to follow screening with two ideas and implement them well. First, you need a good schoolwide discipline plan, one in which behavioral expectations are clear and consistent for all students. All teachers must carefully monitor students' behavior and follow through consistently and calmly with consequences for what they see. The emphasis must be on praise and recognition for desired behavior, not on punishment for transgression (although nonphysical, consistent, reasonable punishment for misbehavior is important). Second, you need good alternatives for the 5 or 6 percent who still misbehave. The plan must involve teaching appropriate conduct, much as one teaches anything else—through direct instruction, guided practice, feedback and praise for making progress. Sometimes, but not always, this can be administered in the context of a regular school and classroom. Sometimes, such instruction needs to be done in a special class or school where the teaching can be more intensive and sustained.

Behavioral screening? Absolutely—but only if we do it right and practice prevention. We can't prevent all problems, but we can improve the odds a lot.

11

Changing Society's Expectations of Boys Can Prevent School Violence

William S. Pollack

William S. Pollack is a clinical psychiatrist and an assistant professor of psychiatry at Harvard Medical School. He is the author of Real Boys: Rescuing Our Sons from the Myths of Masculinity *and* Real Boys' Voices.

A series of school shootings in America has led to an extreme fear of teenage boys. Parents, school administrators, and students are scrutinizing all boys in an attempt to predict who will be the next killers. Boys themselves live in terror not only of the violence that may be perpetrated against them but also of being falsely accused of an intention to commit violence. Some are afraid that they, too, have the potential to become violent. Adding to this problem are society's unspoken rules that encourage boys to be strong and aggressive while hiding their shame and sadness. These rules condition boys to express their pain and rage through violence. In order to stop the violence, schools must create an atmosphere in which teenage boys can express their pain instead of repressing it until it drives them to acts of desperation.

> *"I don't want to be that type of kid who comes to school and just takes out a gun and starts shooting."*
> —Bobby, age 12, from a city in the West

> *"The other day I walked into school and a girl was carrying balloons and one of them popped. Everyone in the whole school got really terrified."*
> —Errol, age 17, from a suburb in the West

William S. Pollack, "The Columbine Syndrome: Boys and the Fear of Violence," *National Forum: Phi Kappa Phi Journal*, vol. 80, Fall 2000, pp. 39–42. Copyright © 2000 by William S. Pollack. Reproduced by permission.

"I think there are people at my school who have the potential for doing something similar."
        —Jules, age 17, from a suburb in the South

"People were coming up to me and begging me not to kill them. I felt like telling them: 'Cut it out; I'm not going to do anything.'"
        —Cody, age 14, from a suburb in New England

"You can't say 'them' or 'you.' You have to say 'us.'"
        —Jimmy, age 16, from a small town in the West

Probably no risk other than violence has made America more afraid of boys and made boys more afraid of *being male* and living in this country. Though it has been understood for decades that the perpetrators of most violent crimes in our nation are male, the recent spate of school shootings, culminating in the heinous massacre of teachers and students recently carried out in suburban Littleton, Colorado [where two students went on a shooting spree, killing thirteen others and themselves], has made the public ever more frightened and confused about the threat of extreme violence and its connection, in particular, with boys. Boys of adolescent age, boys just like the ones who have contributed to my research, are the ones pulling the triggers and injuring, sometimes killing, their peers and school teachers. What many people do not realize—and what the media following Columbine have failed to portray as well as they might—is that most of the *victims* of teenage violence, indeed the vast majority, are also boys.

Consequences of the Columbine Syndrome

In my travels across our country, listening to boys and doing research for my latest book, *Real Boys' Voices*, I have come to see that the effect of these terrifying crimes has been immense. It has led to the "Columbine Syndrome": across our nation students, parents, and teachers are absolutely terrified—sometimes to an extreme degree—about which boys amongst them are violent, who the next perpetrators might be, and who their victims will become. Paranoia is rampant. School children and the adults around them are constantly canvassing the student body and worrying, often inappropriately, that particular students may be murderous. Grady, age seventeen, from a school in the South says, "When a kid's wearing a trenchcoat and he's going for something in his jacket, you learn from watching the news that more than likely he might have a gun."

The consequence is that boys themselves are becoming increasingly afraid. They are frightened not only of being victimized by the rage and violence of other boys, but also of being accused, or falsely accused, of having the disposition it takes to snap into hyper-violent action and embark on a murderous rampage. Boys fear that despite their true nature, they will automatically, because they are boys, be seen as somehow toxic, dangerous, and culpable. As one young preadolescent boy said, "I think women like small kids. Girls like newborn babies. They don't like big people. We bigger guys scare everybody, and then we get blamed even when we've done nothing wrong."

Boys are also afraid of the violence they may feel inside themselves and of whether it is safe to talk with us about it. As they internalize this fear of being misunderstood—and of being charged with having a violent temperament they genuinely do not have—boys themselves are beginning to worry if maybe, just maybe, the demon is within, if lurking underneath their conscious understanding of themselves, are uncontrollable urges to do depraved violent acts. The Columbine Syndrome means that America's boys today are as confused about violence as they are afraid of it. *They fear each other and they fear their own selves.*

The "Boy Code"

While the statistics indicate that teenage boys not only commit a considerable percentage of the nation's violent juvenile crimes but also become the frequent *victims* of those crimes, in reality there seems to be no inherent biological factor that makes boys more violent than their female counterparts. Violence committed by and acted out upon boys seems to stem, more often than not, from what we teach (or do not teach) boys about the behavior we expect from them. It comes from society's set of rules about masculinity, the Boy Code that says, "To be a man, you must show your strength and your power. You must show that you can hold your own if challenged by another male. You can show your rage, but you must not show any other emotions. You must protect your honor and fight off shame at all costs."

Think of it yourself. A boy gets slightly angry as a way to express his pain, and there will be mixed emotions. Some of us may show some fear, but if the anger is in control, we are unlikely to respond in a drastic manner. So long as it is "within bounds," society tends to approve of, if not encourage, aggression by and among boys. Violence in boys is widely (although, as I have said, incorrectly) seen as inevitable, if not biologically pre-ordained. As long as nobody is seriously hurt, no lethal weapons are employed, and especially within the framework of sports and games—football, soccer, boxing, wrestling—aggression and violence are widely accepted and even encouraged in boys. Boys are constantly trying to prove their masculinity through aggression, and society is complicit; winning a game, or even a fight, helps many boys gain society's respect.

Boys themselves are beginning to worry if maybe . . . the demon is within.

The corollary to this message, simply enough, is that soft, gentle, non-violent boys, are "feminine" and therefore losers. While we often pay lip service to helping boys "put feelings into words" and even create multi-million educational programs to address this, if you're "a big guy" and start to express your vulnerable emotions too openly, people crawl back in fear. Or imagine the boy who misses a goal and bursts into tears on the soccer field. He is not considered masculine. Peers call him a "girl," "sissy" or "fag." Parents cringe. It is precisely in this environment that even the most hearty boy soon learns to avoid showing his pain in public. He may want to cry, he may wish he could speak of his fear, sadness, or shame, but he holds it back. He resists. Instead, the boy displays anger, aggression, and violence.

Perhaps it should not shock us, then, when we hear from the boys who say that while they overwhelmingly condemn extreme violence, and to a large extent do not engage in it, they can understand, empathize, with the boys who hit, hurt, and even kill. They tell us about what the teasing and razzing "can do to your head," how alone and isolated some boys can become, and how rage is indeed often the only sanctioned emotion that does not bring further ridicule to them. We are all afraid of boys and violence, but boys, it turns out, are the most in fear. Gun detectors, violence screening tools or *"profiles,"* armed guards, and *"zero tolerance"* only goad our sons into the very aggression we, and they, are afraid of; by expecting boys to be angry, rambunctious, and dangerous, we push boys to fulfill these prophecies. This is the essence, I believe, of the Columbine Syndrome. By living in fear and expecting danger, that is exactly what we produce.

By living in fear and expecting danger, that is exactly what we produce.

To compound the risk to all of us, society is now giving boys another complex and confusing message, what I call the "No Black Shirts" response. Because the Columbine killers were outcast boys, spiteful nonconforming boys who wore dark clothing and were estranged from their peers, society has now rushed to the conclusion that adolescent boys who seem "different," especially ones who seem quiet, distant, and in pain, are the likely perpetrators of the next ghastly Columbine-like crime. Sadly, what the huge majority of outcast boys needs most—in fact what many so-called "popular" boys, boys on the "inside" often desperately need as well—is not to have their pain suppressed and disregarded, but rather to have it listened to and understood.

Curbing the syndrome

Boys in pain require immediate intervention. As soon as we detect that a boy is experiencing emotional distress, we need to stop what we are doing, turn towards him, and hear him out. Whether he is wearing a black hood or Brooks Brothers sweater, whether he is well-liked or an outcast, he needs us to come toward him, embrace and affirm him, and assuage his hurt feelings before they push him to the edge. Boys are simply not inherently violent or dangerous, and the emotional distress that they may feel, in the first instance, does not make them any more so. But if we continue to give boys the message that expressing their distress is forbidden, that we will ignore their vulnerable feelings when we see them, and that we actually expect them to act out angrily and violently, we should not be surprised that the world becomes, for all of us, a mighty frightful place.

As the voices I heard (sampled in brief above) and published in detail in *Real Boys' Voices* exemplify only a tiny percentage of boys are capable of egregious acts of violence. In truth, as aggressive as they can perhaps be pushed to become, most boys are quite anxious about and revolted by the prevalence of violence in society. They feel powerless to do anything about it, though, because they simply feel too much shame, too concerned about how other people will respond to their confessions of fear.

The solution, I believe, is for society to commit to a whole new way of seeing boys and violence. First, as a society we need to decide, unequivocally, that as much as we will not exalt boys who fight, we also will not punish or ostracize those who show their vulnerability. By defending and actually providing positive reinforcement to boys who openly exhibit their moments of fear, longing, anxiety, and despair, by telling these boys and men that they are fully "masculine" no matter what emotions they share with us, we can help them avoid the repression and resistance that may make them bottle up their emotions and then spill them out in irrational acts. Second, because society may not change overnight, we need to be on the lookout for the signs of sadness and depression that in boys and men so often seem harder to see, or more difficult to believe and accept. In my book, I outlined these many signs. If we are attentive to them, and if we help boys overcome the pain and disaffection that gives rise to them, much of the aggression and violence we now see will evaporate, or be directed towards safe, appropriate channels.

Finally, we must simply decide, as a society, that most boys, as angry or aggressive as they may become, are highly unlikely to become dangerous in any way. The boys' voices quoted at the beginning of this piece are overwhelming proof that most of our sons have a non-violent nature and that, in reality, their greater struggle is with sadness and the fear of violence rather than with violence itself. Together we must create prophecies that their gentle nature will triumph over old pressures to act tough and lash out. Perhaps if we hear boys' fears about violence in a new light, read their stories with a new empathy, we may be able to reach across the boundaries of fear and create a new dialogue of peace. For boys and for the rest of us, the only cure for the Columbine Syndrome, in the end, is to develop safe spaces that are friendly to boys and thereby create genuine security. The time is now!

12

Restoring God to American Culture Is the Only Way to Prevent School Violence

George A. Kendall

George A. Kendall received his MA in sociology from the University of Detroit. He is a freelance writer and philosopher.

In the wake of school shootings, liberals have called on the public to sympathize with the killers and have advocated more gun control, school counselors, and government programs as ways to reduce youth violence. All of these proposals fail to acknowledge that the true cause of the violence is the exclusion of God from schools and the culture at large. This rejection of God has created a culture devoid of spiritual meaning in which young people are encouraged to embrace chaos, violence, and death. School violence can only end if the culture rejects liberal beliefs and adopts spiritual values.

One bit of "collateral damage" from the school shootings in Colorado[1] is that our liberal elites gained still another opportunity to put their stupidity and arrogance on display. Indeed, the level of inanity has been truly astonishing. One particularly egregious moron who was interviewed on National Public Radio (where else?) could not stop going on about how when young people are "disenfranchised" from the system, they may be tempted to act out in violent ways. For heaven's sake, who isn't disenfranchised? Who isn't alienated? When people live under a regime as irrational and destructive as the one we live under, any sane person is going to detest that regime. That doesn't mean you go around shooting people, though.

And of course everyone from the sociopath-in-chief [a reference to then-president Bill Clinton] on down is keeping us supplied with pious

---

1. In April 1999 students Eric Harris and Dylan Klebold went on a shooting rampage at Columbine High School in Littleton, Colorado, killing twelve students, one teacher, and themselves.

George A. Kendall, "School Violence and Clueless Liberals," *Wanderer*, May 6, 1999. Copyright © 1999 by George A. Kendall. Reproduced by permission of the author.

nostrums about the need to be on the alert for the early warning signs of violence in young people, the importance of parents spending time with their children, why we need more school counselors and psychologists, and so on, ad nauseam. The First Harpy [a reference to then–First Lady Hillary Clinton] has announced a war on youth violence, something which does rather little to reassure me.

The sentimentalism is endless. When we are told that our hearts should go out, not only to the families of the victims, but to the families of the killers, I begin to find it difficult to keep my lunch down. The families of the killers may well be guilty of criminal negligence; they should be investigated and, if need be, prosecuted. I can imagine no way a parent could have his or her son collecting weapons on the scale these two were or making bombs on such a scale, and have no idea that anything was going on. (On the other hand, I find it a bit ridiculous when we are simplistically told that students who heard the killers make threatening remarks should have gone to the authorities—everyone knows that if you go to the authorities with things like that, not only will nothing be done, but you are likely to be vilified for making trouble. This is rather like the advice sometimes given to orthodox Catholics that when you see liturgical abuses in your parish, you should contact the bishop. Yeah, right! We all know how far that gets you.)

Needless to say, the usual chorus of pleas for gun control is being heard. Nobody but us right-wing, extremists seems to be suggesting that maybe if the teachers in that school had been armed, the outcome of the whole incident might have been different.

Shutting God out

What this catalog of idiocies comes down to is the inability of liberal ideologues to deal with spiritual evil. And that is indeed what is in question here. One person I heard from on the Internet on this whole subject suggested that if we exclude God from the schools, we are bound to let Satan in. I agree, but would add that it is not just the schools—it is our whole civilization which has shut God out, and when we do that, we let Satan in. No one can live in a spiritual vacuum. If we remove God from our culture, we create a space for the demonic. When we attack and ridicule and eliminate the sources of moral, social, and spiritual order, people are going to embrace chaos.

And, indeed, if we look at the horrors of today's youth culture—the drugs, the sexual promiscuity, MTV, Marilyn Manson, the recent fads involving body piercing and mutilation—it is hard to escape the conclusion that our young people have in truth embraced chaos. Harris and Klebold are probably only the tip of the iceberg when it comes to young people who are capable of violence. When you grow up in a culture whose elites have done everything in their power to reduce it to a spiritual vacuum, you are bound to know, however obscurely, that you have been deprived of something precious, something you need more than the air that you breathe, and the result is a rage that can turn to homicide or suicide, or both, as in the present case. (Isn't it interesting that one of the killers was named after [folk/rock singer] Bob Dylan, so much an icon of the spiritually destructive sixties generation?)

But, of course, the liberal elites just give you a blank stare if you try to point any of this out. They know better. They know that school violence and other evils occur because their social engineering programs are not quite working at maximum efficiency yet. A little more fine-tuning will take care of everything. It's all a matter of better management—more government programs, more counselors, and, of course, gun control. And don't forget "hate crimes" laws.

If we exclude God from the schools, we are bound to let Satan in.

None of them seem able to see that the violence they deplore is in fact the natural effect of the culture of death which they themselves have been forcing down everyone's throat—not just in America, but throughout the world. A culture that pushes abortion, contraception, and euthanasia so avidly is telling young people in many, many ways that life—including their own—is worthless. While I was watching CNN (probably a mistake) before writing this, I saw a picture of one of the young women who was killed. My immediate reaction to it was, "She's so pretty! Why would anyone do that to her?" It seemed like such an attack on the beauty of God's creation. And yet our elites have worked night and day for so long now to teach us to hate the creation. What else can they expect?

But there is no limit to their hypocrisy. Not only are they willing or unable to admit their own complicity in evil, but they are all so very sanctimonious when they deplore evil. It is obvious that when things like this happen, our liberals see themselves as too highly evolved to be capable of violence, and so they approach it all in a kind of atmosphere of moral earnestness and liberal Protestant high-mindedness that is truly sickening. They see themselves as the representatives of the higher liberal culture, trying so earnestly to assist the masses of less advanced, less enlightened people who engage in such things as murder, domestic abuse, homophobia. They are assuming the white man's burden and are obviously very pleased with themselves for doing so, even in the midst of tragedies as appalling as the one in Colorado.

Quite a bit earlier in this century, [philosopher of history] Eric Voegelin had this to say about our ruling elites:

"Gnostic societies and their leaders will recognize dangers to their existence when they develop, but such dangers will not be met by appropriate actions in the world of reality. They will rather be met by magic operations in the dream world, such as disapproval, moral condemnation, declarations of intention, resolutions, . . . etc. The intellectual and moral corruption which expresses itself in the aggregate of such magic operations may pervade a society with the weird, ghostly atmosphere of a lunatic asylum."

It is certainly a threat to the existence of a society when the younger generation is rushing headlong into the abyss, like the Gadarene swine. And when the only response the elders can come up with is the kind of mindless sloganeering (magic incantations) they have been spewing out since the school shootings, we are definitely living in a lunatic asylum. God help us!

Organizations to Contact

The editors have compiled the following list of organizations concerned with the issues presented in this book. The descriptions are derived from materials provided by the organizations. All have publications or information available for interested readers. The list was compiled on the date of publication of the present volume; the information provided here may change. Be aware that many organizations take several weeks or longer to respond to inquiries, so allow as much time as possible.

American Academy of Child and Adolescent Psychiatry (AACAP)
3615 Wisconsin Ave. NW, Washington, DC 20016-3007
(202) 966-7300 • fax: (202) 966-2891
Web site: www.aacap.org

AACAP is the leading national professional medical association committed to treating the 7 to 12 million American youth suffering from mental, behavioral, and developmental disorders. It publishes the monthly *Journal of the American Academy of Child and Adolescent Psychiatry* and the fact sheets "Children and TV Violence," "Understanding Violent Behavior in Children and Adolescents," and "Children's Threats: When Are They Serious?"

American Civil Liberties Union (ACLU)
125 Broad St., Eighteenth Fl., New York, NY 10004
(212) 549-2500 • fax: (212) 549-2646
Web site: www.aclu.org

The ACLU is a national organization that works to defend Americans' civil rights as guaranteed by the U.S. Constitution. It works to establish equality before the law, regardless of race, color, sexual orientation, or national origin. The ACLU publishes and distributes the semiannual newsletter *Civil Liberties Alert*, policy statements, pamphlets, and reports.

Canadians Concerned About Violence in Entertainment (C-CAVE)
167 Glen Rd., Toronto, ON M4W 2W8 Canada
(416) 961-0853 • fax: (416) 929-2720
Web site: www.c-cave.com • e-mail: info@c-cave.com

C-CAVE conducts research on the harmful effects violence in the media has on society and provides its findings to the Canadian government and public. The organization's committees research issues of violence against women and children, sports violence, and pornography. C-CAVE disseminates educational materials, including periodic news updates and the book *Mind Abuse: Media Violence in an Information Age*.

Center for the Prevention of School Violence
1801 Mail Service Center, Raleigh, NC 27699-1801
800-299-6054 • 919-733-3388 ext. 332
e-mail: jaclyn.myers@ncmail.net • Web site: www.ncdjjdp.org/cpsv

The Center for the Prevention of School Violence is a primary point of contact for information, programs, and research about school violence and its prevention. As a clearinghouse, it provides information about all aspects of the problems which fall under the heading of school violence as well as information about strategies that are directed at solving these problems.

Mediascope

100 Universal City Plaza, Bldg. 6159, Universal City, CA 91608
(818) 733-3180 • fax: (818) 733-3181
e-mail: facts@mediascope.org • Web site: www.mediascope.org

Mediascope is a national, nonprofit research and public policy organization working to raise awareness about the way media affects society. Founded in 1992, it encourages responsible depictions of social and health issues in film, television, the Internet, video games, advertising, and music. Among its many publications are the issue brief *Crime and Violence in American Schools* and the report "National Television Violence Study."

Morality in Media (MIM)

475 Riverside Dr., Ste. 239, New York, NY 10115
(212) 870-3222 • fax: (212) 870-2765
e-mail: mim@moralityinmedia.org • Web site: www.moralityinmedia.org

Established in 1962, MIM is a national, not-for-profit interfaith organization that works to combat obscenity and violence and to uphold decency standards in the media. It maintains the National Obscenity Law Center, a clearinghouse of legal materials, and conducts public information programs to involve concerned citizens. Its publications include the bimonthly *Morality in Media* newsletter and the handbook *TV: The World's Greatest Mind-Bender*.

National Alliance for Safe Schools (NASS)

PO Box 290, Slanesville, WV 25445
(888) 510-6500 • (304) 496-8100 • fax: (304) 496-8105
e-mail: nass@raven-villages.net • Web site: www.safeschools.org

Founded in 1977 by a group of school security directors, the National Alliance for Safe Schools was established to provide training, security assessments, and technical assistance to school districts interested in reducing school-based crime and violence. It publishes the book *Making Schools Safe for Students*.

National Association of School Resource Officers (NASRO)

PO Box 39, Osprey, FL 34229-0039
(888) 31-NASRO
e-mail: resourcer@aol.com • Web site: www.nasro.org

The National Association of School Resource Officers is the first and only nonprofit training organization made up of liaison officers currently assigned to a school community. Its mission is to break down the barriers between law enforcement and youth by establishing better communication about the legal system. Its official publication is *Resourcer*.

National Institute of Justice (NIJ)
National Criminal Justice Reference Service (NCJRS)

PO Box 6000, Rockville, MD 20849-6000
(800) 851-3420 • (301) 519-5500
e-mail: askncjrs@ncjrs.org • Web site: www.ncjrs.org

A component of the Office of Justice Programs of the U.S. Department of Justice, the NIJ supports research on crime, criminal behavior, and crime prevention. The National Criminal Justice Reference Service acts as a clearinghouse for criminal justice information for researchers and other interested individuals. Among the numerous reports it publishes and distributes are "Addressing Bullying in Schools: Theory and Practice," "Crime in the Schools: Reducing Conflict with Student Problem Solving," and "Preventing School Shootings: A Summary of a U.S. Secret Service School Initiative Report."

National School Safety Center (NSSC)
141 Duesenberg Dr., Ste. 11, Westlake Village, CA 91362
(805) 373-9977 • fax: (805) 373-9277
e-mail: info@nsscl.org • Web site: www.nsscl.org

The NSSC is a research organization that studies school crime and violence, including hate crimes. The center's mandate is to focus national attention on cooperative solutions to problems that disrupt the educational process. NSSC provides training, technical assistance, legal and legislative aid, and publications and films toward this cause. Its resources include the books *Set Straight on Bullies* and *Gangs in Schools: Breaking Up Is Hard to Do* and the newsletter *School Safety Update*, which is published nine times a year.

Office of Juvenile Justice and Delinquency Prevention (OJJDP)
810 Seventh St. NW, Washington, DC 20531
(202) 307-5911 • fax: (202) 307-2093
e-mail: askjj@ojp.usdoj.gov • Web site: http://ojjdp.ncjrs.org

As the primary federal agency charged with monitoring and improving the juvenile justice system, the OJJDP develops and funds programs on juvenile justice. Among its goals are the prevention and control of illegal drug use and serious crime by juveniles. Through its Juvenile Justice Clearinghouse, the OJJDP distributes fact sheets such as Addressing the Problem of Juvenile Bullying and reports, including an annual report on school safety.

The Oregon Social Learning Center (OSLC)
160 E. Fourth Ave., Eugene, OR 97401
(541) 485-2711 • fax: (541) 485-7087
e-mail: kathyj@oslc.org • Web site: www.oslc.org

OSLC is a nonprofit, independent research center dedicated to finding ways to help children and parents as they cope with daily problems. The center is known for its successful work in designing and implementing interventions for children and parents to help encourage successful adjustment and discourage aggressive behaviors within the family, the school, and the community. OSLC has published more than four hundred articles in scientific journals, written more than two hundred chapters in textbooks about children and adolescents and their families, published eleven books, and made many films, videotapes, and audiotapes on parenting.

Partnerships Against Violence Network (PAVNET) Online
(301) 504-5462
e-mail: jgladsto@nalusda.gov • Web site: www.pavnet.org

PAVNET Online is a virtual library of information about violence and at-risk youths, representing data from seven different federal agencies. Its programs promote the prevention of youth violence through education as well as through sports and recreation. Among PAVNET's curricula publications are *Creative Conflict Solving for Kids* and *Escalating Violence: The Impact of Peers*. The monthly *PAVNET Online* newsletter is also available at its Web site.

Safe Schools and Violence Prevention Office (SSVPO)
California Department of Education
1430 N St., Sacramento, CA 95814
(916) 319-0800
Web site: www.cde.ca.gov/spbranch/safety

Operated by the California Department of Education, SSVPO offers assistance, training, materials, as well as supporting grant programs to foster the development of safe schools and communities. Its programs include counseling and guidance, conflict resolution and youth mediation, hate-motivated behavior violence prevention, high-risk youth education, gang risk intervention, and school/law enforcement partnership. SSVPO's publications include *Safe Schools: A Planning Guide for Action, On Alert: Gang Prevention—School In-Service Guidelines* and *Hate-Motivated Behavior in Schools*.

U.S. Department of Education
Safe and Drug-Free Schools Program
400 Maryland Ave. SW, Washington, DC 20202
(800) USA-LEARN • (202) 260-3954 • fax: (202) 401-0689
e-mail: customerservice@inet.ed.gov • Web site: www.ed.gov

The Safe and Drug-Free Schools Program is the U.S. Department of Education's primary vehicle for reducing violence and drug, alcohol, and tobacco use through education and prevention activities in America's schools. It publishes the reports "Threat Assessment in Schools: A Guide to Managing Threatening Situations and to Creating Safe School Climates" and "Student-led Crime Prevention: A Real Resource with Powerful Promise."

Youth Crime Watch of America (YCWA)
9200 S. Dadeland Blvd., Ste. 417, Miami, FL 33156
(305) 670-2409 • fax: (305) 670-3805
e-mail: ycwa@ycwa.org • Web site: www.ycwa.org

Youth Crime Watch of America is a nonprofit organization that assists youth in actively reducing crime and drug use in their schools and communities. Its resources include handbooks for adult advisers and youth on starting and operating a Youth Crime Watch program, a *Getting Started* video, a *Mentoring Activities* handbook, and a *Talking with Youth About Prevention* teaching guide.

Bibliography

Books

Elliot Aaronson	*Nobody Left to Hate: Teaching Compassion After Columbine.* New York: Worth Publishers, 2000.
Michael Bochenek	*Hatred in the Hallways: Violence and Discrimination Against Lesbian, Gay, Bisexual, and Transgender Students in U.S. Schools.* New York: Human Rights Watch, 2001.
Ronnie Casella	*At Zero Tolerance: Punishment, Prevention, and School Violence.* New York: Peter Lang, 2001.
Doriane Lambelet Coleman	*Fixing Columbine: The Challenge to American Liberalism.* Durham, NC: Carolina Academic Press, 2002.
Raymond B. Flannery Jr.	*Preventing Youth Violence: A Guide for Parents, Teachers, and Counselors.* New York: Continuum, 1999.
SuEllen Fried and Paula Fried	*Bullies and Victims: Helping Your Child Survive the Schoolyard Battlefield.* New York: M. Evans and Company, 1996.
Dave Grossman and Gloria DeGaetano	*Stop Teaching Our Kids to Kill: A Call to Action Against TV, Movie, and Video Game Violence.* New York: Crown, 1999.
Kathleen M. Heide	*Young Killers: The Challenge of Juvenile Homicide.* Thousand Oaks, CA: Sage, 2000.
William G. Hinkle and Stuart Henry, eds.	*School Violence.* Thousand Oaks, CA: Sage, 2000.
Allan M. Hoffman, ed.	*Schools, Violence, and Society.* Westport, CT: Praeger, 1996.
Bob Larson	*Extreme Evil: Kids Killing Kids.* Nashville: T. Nelson Publishers, 1999.
Richard Lawrence	*School Crime and Juvenile Justice.* New York: Oxford University Press, 1997.
Joy D. Osofsky, ed.	*Children in a Violent Society.* New York: Guilford Press, 1997.
Ted Schwartz	*Kids and Guns: The History, the Present, the Dangers, and the Remedies.* New York: Franklin Watts, 1999.
Mohammad Shafii and Sharon Lee Shafii, eds.	*School Violence: Assessment, Management, Prevention.* Washington, DC: American Psychiatric Publishers, 2001.
James E. Shaw	*Jack and Jill, Why They Kill: Saving Our Children, Saving Ourselves.* Seattle: Onjinjinkta Publishers, 2000.

Peter L. Sheras — *Your Child: Bully or Victim? Understanding and Ending School Yard Tyranny.* New York: Fireside, 2002.

Periodicals

Giant Abutalebi Aryani, Carl L. Alsabrook, and Terry D. Garrett — "Scholastic Crime Stoppers," *FBI Law Enforcement Bulletin*, September 2001.

Mark Anderson et al. — "School-Associated Violent Deaths in the United States, 1994–1999," *Journal of the American Medical Association*, December 5, 2001.

Dale Anema — "A Father at Columbine High," *American Enterprise*, September 1999.

Sandy Banks — "Recovery from Shootings Starts with Stopping Bullies," *Los Angeles Times*, March 13, 2001.

Joel Best — "Monster Hype: How a Few Isolated Tragedies—and Their Supposed Causes—Were Turned into a National 'Epidemic,'" *Education Next*, Summer 2002.

Katherine T. Bucher and M. Lee Manning — "Challenges and Suggestions for Safe Schools," *Clearing House*, January/February 2003.

John Buell — "Alternative Perspectives on School Violence," *Humanist*, September 2001.

Janis R. Bullock — "Bullying Among Children," *Childhood Education*, Spring 2002.

Mary Eberstadt — "Home-Alone America," *Policy Review*, June 2001.

Annette Fuentes — "Discipline and Punish: Zero Tolerance Policies Have Created a 'Lockdown Environment' in Schools," *Nation*, December 15, 2003.

Henry A. Giroux — "Zero Tolerance," *Tikkun*, March 2001.

Carey Goldberg — "For Those Who Dress Differently, an Increase in Being Viewed as Abnormal," *New York Times*, May 1, 1999.

Francis Q. Hoang — "Addressing School Violence," *FBI Law Enforcement Bulletin*, August 2001.

Gayle Holten — "Time to Take Bullying of Children More Seriously," *Cincinnati Post*, April 27, 2001.

Andrew Hudgins — "When Bullies Ruled the Hallways," *New York Times*, May 1, 1999.

Richard Jerome — "Disarming the Rage," *People Weekly*, June 4, 2001.

Rachel Jupin — "Someone to Lean On: Violence in Schools May Be Prevented If Students Know They Have Teachers They Can Turn To for Comfort and Advice," *NEM Today*, April 2002.

Gary Kleck — "School Lesson: Armed Self-Defense Works," *Wall Street Journal*, March 27, 2001.

SHELBYVILLE-SHELBY COUNTY
PUBLIC LIBRARY

Frank Kogan	"Everyday Terror in the Suburbs South of Denver," *Village Voice*, May 4, 1999.
Dave Kopel	"Zero Good Sense," *National Review*, June 6, 2001.
John Leo	"Dubious Definitions Undercut Anti-Bullying Movement," *Seattle Times*, May 15, 2001.
Mike Males	"School Shootings," *Los Angeles Times*, March 11, 2001.
Al Martinez	"Looking for a Scapegoat: The Elusive School Bully," *Los Angeles Times*, March 29, 2001.
Susan Meadows	"Ghosts of Columbine," *Newsweek*, November 3, 2003.
Frank Morriss	"The Why Must Be Found Within Us," *Wanderer*, April 29, 1999.
New York Times	"Columbine Students Talk of the Disaster and Life," April 30, 1999.
Peggy Noonan	"The Culture of Death," *Wall Street Journal*, April 22, 1999.
Kelly Patricia O'Meara	"A Prescription for Violence?" *Insight on the News*, May 21, 2001.
Reece L. Peterson and Russell Skiba	"Creating School Climates That Prevent School Violence," *Social Studies*, July 2001.
Darrell Scott	"Columbine Tragedy Shows Nation Must Return to a Trust in God," *Insight on the News*, May 1, 2001.
Jane Shackford	"A Compulsion to Repeat Failure," *Humanist*, September 2001.
Jane Spencer	"Caught in the WAVE: A Corporate Antiviolence Program Targets Students Who Don't Fit In," *Nation*, December 4, 2000.
Jackson Toby	"Let Them Drop Out," *Weekly Standard*, April 9, 2001.
Suzanne Tochterman	"From Horror to Healing: How Columbine Impacted Students," *Reclaiming Children and Youth*, Winter 2002.
Peter Wilkinson	"Humiliation and Revenge: The Story of Reb and VoDkA," *Rolling Stone*, June 10, 1999.

Index